women for hire's

Get-Ahead Guide to Career Success

women for hire's

Get-Ahead Guide to Career Success

Tory Johnson

Robyn Freedman Spizman

A Perigee Book

A Perigee Book
Published by The Berkley Publishing Group
A division of Penguin Group (USA) Inc.
375 Hudson Street
New York, New York 10014

Copyright © 2004 by Women For Hire LLC and
Robyn Freedman Spizman Literary Works LLC
Cover design by Ben Gibson
Text design by Kristin del Rosario

Perigee trade paperback edition: September 2004

Visit our website at www.penguin.com

Library of Congress Cataloging-in-Publication Data

Johnson, Tory.
    Women for hire's get-ahead guide to career success / Tory Johnson and Robyn Freedman
Spizman.—1st Perigee pbk. ed.
        p. cm.
    ISBN 0-399-53017-7
    1. Vocational guidance for women. 2. Career development. 3. Women—Employment. I.
Title: Get-ahead guide to career success. II. Spizman, Robyn Freedman. III. Title.

HF5382.6.J64 2004
650.14'082—dc22   2004044486

Printed in the United States of America
10 9 8 7 6 5 4 3 2 1

We continue to salute hardworking women past, present, and future. Apply the advice and information on these pages to unleash your potential and advance your career.

CONTENTS

ACKNOWLEDGMENTS

We extend our greatest thanks to the women and men who went to work for us by sharing their knowledge and insights and whose advice appears throughout the book. To our dedicated literary agent, Meredith Bernstein, who supported our vision of our first book, *Women For Hire: The Ultimate Guide to Getting a Job,* and then helped make this second book a reality. To our passionate editor, Michelle Howry, for her enthusiasm, encouragement, and exceptional eye, and the entire team at Penguin Putnam, including copyeditor, Erica Rose, and especially Perigee publisher, John Duff, for continuing to embrace Women For Hire. To the hundreds of recruiters and human resource professionals—and the thousands of women who attend the Women For Hire events, thank you for making our network stronger each year.

From Tory Johnson: To my husband, Peter, and our children, Emma, Jake, and Nick. Your unconditional love and laughter is the best fuel for this working girl. To Stephanie Biasi, Ingrid Brodegaard, Dora Dvir, Lara Hall, and Jami Schievelbein for your gossip breaks, lunch order debates, and genuine passion for what we do. A big thanks to Mordecai Budner, Rachel Tarlow Gul, Jennifer Richards, and Beverly Walters. To David Beilinson, Jodi Goldman, Julie Stein, Natasha Gregson Wagner, Lindsay Weitz, and Julie Zerring—your friendship, support, and occasional ribbing are always a pleasure. To Sherry Beilinson, Evelyn Goldstein, and Donna Weitz, whose humor and hard work help make it all possible. And finally to Reba Amdur, Nola Firestone, Phyllis Goldfarb, Marvin Michael, Frank Redican, Lisa Revesz, Gaylen Robbins, Samantha Steinberg, Sandy Steinberg, Ken Weitz, and especially Randy Green for your exceptional advice—I'm fortunate to have all of you by my side.

From Robyn Freedman Spizman: To my husband, Willy, and our children, Justin and Ali, who support me in all of my literary endeavors and continue to make my work worthwhile, huge hugs and my endless appreciation. I have enormous appreciation also for my wonderful family, especially my dedicated parents, Phyllis and Jack Freedman, who made sure I knew I could do anything I put my mind to. To Doug and Genie Freedman, Dr. Sam Spizman and Gena Gold, Lois and Jerry Blonder, and Ramona Freedman for being the best peanut gallery anyone could ask for and cheering me on at every turn. And to Bettye Storne who is my right arm and household angel. To the talented Suzi Brozman for your wonderful assistance and The Spizman Agency for your ongoing support. A "perfect hair day" thank you to Jack Morton of Indulgence Salon for your masterful expertise, and lastly a world of thanks to my circle of close friends, family, co-workers, and the amazing individuals I've worked with throughout time who have inspired me. I continue to count my lucky stars, and my good fortune in life is thanks to all of you.

PREFACE

In October 2001, just a month after the horrendous terrorist attacks of September 11, Women For Hire held one of its largest career expos ever in New York. Nearly seventy leading employers committed to recruiting at this event, which was no small feat given the economic beating the city took in the wake of the collapse of the Twin Towers.

In the midst of the normal chaos of finalizing every detail the day before an event, I received a surprise phone call from President Bill Clinton. After I got over the initial shock that it wasn't just my husband playing a crazy joke, I listened as the former President congratulated me on Women For Hire's success. He reminded me that at the core of our freedom and financial independence in this country is the right to work. He encouraged me to keep up the hard work. All that in under a minute.

When I share this anecdote with other professional women, there are always two distinct responses: half of them say to me, "You go, girl! Good for you. Regardless of your political preference, a call from an American president is very exciting." Of course I'm thrilled by those kind words.

The other reaction isn't as nice. They look at me as if to say, "My, my, my, doesn't Tory think she's quite pleased with herself to brag about this phone call." That always startles me and I've never grown comfortable with accepting that I'm out of bounds or conceited for telling my story.

The fact is I should be proud of my accomplishments in founding a company that has served more than 100,000 professional women and more than one thousand employers in a range of fields. If I was shy or timid about sharing Women For Hire's successes, it would be impossible for us to help other women in their quest for advancement. Through our career expos, group seminars, and private coaching sessions, we encourage all women to find their own "President Clinton" moments because, whether serving burgers or designing computers, every working girl must feel comfortable touting her proudest achievements.

My co-author, Robyn Freedman Spizman, shares my passion for empowering women. After our first book, *Women For Hire: The Ultimate Guide to Getting a Job,* which we co-wrote with Lindsey Pollak, was published, we traveled throughout the country offering our insights and advice. We listened to the concerns of professionals as they shared their personal stories of cutbacks, pink slips, and how high unemployment rates impacted everything from their self-esteem to their savings accounts. Not only did we witness women's aversion to networking, a discomfort with self-promotion, and a fear of negotiation, but we also saw firsthand how experienced professionals without college degrees are quick to dismiss their depth of accomplishments and how women in the midst of divorce believe their personal crises diminish their professional worth. These are major hurdles to overcome if a woman is to find the success she deserves.

We also heard from women who avoided layoffs and wanted to know more about achieving balance on the job and after hours. It's not always easy to plot new goals, cope with less than congenial colleagues, and juggle a full load at home. Robyn and I went to work on your behalf to deliver a variety of methods and advice on how to not only survive, but more importantly how to thrive. Throughout this book you'll learn the winning ways of women at all levels in a range of fields. It is our hope their experiences will inspire your own.

Since everyone defines success on their own terms, we wish for you whatever it is that you may dream of for yourself. We're proud to play even a tiny part in your journey. Be gutsy and stay confident!

Tory Johnson
Founder and CEO, Women For Hire

INTRODUCTION

Career success is not just about finding the right job. It is how you think and act, and what you say (and sometimes don't say) that can make or break your career. It is the crossroads of hard work, determination, and opportunity. Your career should be a challenge, but not an insurmountable one. It is a journey with many twists, turns, and changes. This book is intended to be a compass to guide you through the maze. Among the topics to help you get ahead, we will address:

- **Attitude.** Approaching your career with a positive attitude and enthusiasm may sound incredibly simple, but it's the first step in achieving career success. Learn to define success on your own terms, and use this definition to set your career goals.

- **Reinvention.** We all face obstacles and challenges in life, but don't let them paralyze your career. Learn from them and grow stronger, instead of using them as a crutch or safety net for accepting defeat. Take what you've learned, brush yourself off, and reevaluate what you want. Whether you are bored or your circumstances have changed, be gutsy enough to take the leap to a new path.

- **Pulling it all together.** It isn't always good enough to be good enough for the position. To really succeed in your career, you have to go above and beyond. Go back to school, get certified, take on a leadership role, and know your industry inside and out. Don't forget to polish your manners. Business etiquette is back in a big way, yet many professionals are rusty from years of letting formality slide.

- **Behavior.** As you advance in your career, your day-to-day demeanor will become as important as your skills, experience, and talent. It isn't just what you do, it's how you do it. Keep control of your emotions, communicate effectively, and strengthen your leadership skills. Not only must you monitor your own performance, a savvy professional knows how to deal appropriately with the sometimes-destructive habits of others as well.

- **Rubbing elbows.** Other people can do wonders for advancing your career, but rarely will they extend a helping hand unless you ask. Learn to promote yourself and your accomplishments to show others just how worthy you are of their attention. Network your way up.

- **Getting the rewards you deserve.** Money isn't the only reward you derive from your career, but isn't it a big one? Learn to negotiate the salary and benefits you deserve—from retirement savings to telecommuting, the opportunities are limitless. Know your options and create the package that fits *your* needs.

Our last book, *Women For Hire: The Ultimate Guide to Getting a Job,* helped you land the offer. This book, *Women For Hire's Get-Ahead Guide to Career Success,* will help you succeed on the job and get ahead in *all* aspects of your career—from making new contacts, improving your performance, and developing leadership skills, to asking for a raise, negotiating family time, and earning a promotion. The book will help you recognize your success along the way, and adjust your goals, or even your path, as necessary.

We've gathered advice from senior executives, industry experts, and women just like you. From their anecdotes, we've compiled a collection of tips, interactive exercises, resources, and real-life examples, all intended to help you in your career choices and obstacles. Throughout the book, we've inserted sidebars. "It Works for Me" highlight the tools others used to get ahead. "Pitfalls to Ponder" encourage you to learn from other people's mistakes. And "Book Breaks" feature our top picks and recommended reading from successful professionals who tout the titles that have inspired them.

As you grow in your career, take time to celebrate your successes. The last section of this book is dedicated to sharing success stories of women from all professions and the specific steps they took to get where they wanted to be.

CHAPTER ONE

You Are What You Think
Confidence Is the First Step to Success

"I have never heard a man described as 'lucky,' and yet in my career I have been told millions of times how 'lucky' I have been. Women who have achieved are not lucky. We are lucky if we don't fall out of the sky in an airplane or if a plank doesn't hit us in the head. But at work we are ballsy, hardworking. We are magnificent."

—SHEILA NEVINS,
Executive vice president of original programming for HBO

The first step towards career success is being in the right frame of mind. You must believe it in order to achieve it. Since the power of positive thinking can propel your career forward in any direction you dream, you must begin your journey by promising to be optimistic and believing in your own ability to reach beyond your current situation.

Close your eyes and picture the next step. Whether you define success as an entry-level professional in a new field, or the first female CEO of your corporation, it won't happen until you imagine it. Think of the most successful person you've ever heard of. More than likely, she spent years dreaming and plotting and planting the right seeds to make her ideas a reality, from a local business owner to a corporate executive. So start dreaming about your own professional destination. What does success mean to you? What do you want to do and where do you want to be?

A big part of success is learning to think like a successful professional. But for many women, thinking successfully doesn't come naturally; it's a learned process. In this chapter, you'll learn how to define what success means to *you*, then start to make a plan to turn those dreams into reality.

Define Success

CREATE YOUR OWN DEFINITION

Women who really succeed have a clear vision of success and what it means to them. For one woman success is having her own company and being self-sufficient. For another, success is financial rewards for doing something she really loves. And for another, it's a prestigious title, parking space, and corner office. Understanding what success means to you is key. Once you have a personal definition of success, you can use it to weigh career decisions, as motivation to make changes, and as a barometer for measuring how far you've come.

- **Consider your current model for success.** If you haven't previously determined your own definition of success, chances are you are living by someone else's model. Ideas of success are thrown at us from all angles—from our parents and friends to society, school, co-workers, and spouses. Everyone has an idea or formula for success. Is your current idea of success making you happy? You may have adopted the definition that success includes 2.4 children, a white picket fence, and backyard in the suburbs. You may have internalized the idea that success comes with a certain title, such as Doctor or Attorney-at-Law, or with a six-figure salary. It's important to understand your current model for success and question it. Many people follow one path to success only to find out they are not happy when they get there. This is a potential indication that the path to success they followed was not their own.

- **Think about alternative definitions of success.** Once you've determined what path you're on, take a good look at other alternatives.

What are the advantages and disadvantages of each? Maybe defining success as finding inner peace has the advantage of a relatively stress-free lifestyle, but will it provide you with the material things in life you want and fulfill your competitive drive and ambitious nature?

• **Determine whether to stick with your current model of success, or adopt a new one.** Ask yourself some important questions. What is most important in your life? What has made you feel successful in the past? Would you rather have more free time, or more money? Would you rather travel or own your own home? Do you love your job? Are you excited to pursue more advanced positions in your industry?

• **Don't be afraid to accept your new definition of success.** You may have been well on your way to becoming an accountant, only to find you'd rather start a craft business. Of course you have to think things through first, but don't be afraid to take the plunge. Trust yourself.

• **Study success.** If you could trade jobs with someone right now, who would she be? How did she get there? Read articles in newspapers and magazines. Watch for successful women on television; study their confidence and mannerisms, even their vocabulary and style. Load up on quotes and people who inspire you and get to know successful women in your field. The more role models you have, the more motivated you will be to reach for the stars. Your motto? *If she can do it, so can I.*

It's all in the details, and the details are right there, in front of your eyes, in every successful woman you see or meet. Success is an ongoing process that takes time, skills, and relentless determination.

Practice Thinking Positively

Positive thinking can be harder than it seems. Most of us let "reality" squash our career dreams before they've even had a chance to develop. You think of how nice it would be to go for your master's degree, but

before you can even envision yourself in a cap and gown, you come up with a million reasons why you can't do it. Maybe you don't have enough time or money. Or you think you should wait until the kids are grown. Or you can't afford to cut back on work hours. Instead of listing all the reasons you *can't* do something, just this once, list all the reasons you can, and should. Maybe a master's will increase earning potential, open up exciting new career options, or will enable you to better provide for your children's future.

Positive thinking takes practice. We all have negative thoughts from time to time, but it's possible to turn your negative thoughts into positive ones by following these simple guidelines.

- **Identify your negative thoughts.** Negative ideas can spring into your mind so fast and so often that you are hardly even aware of them anymore. Consider the last dream or idea you rejected. Maybe you thought about asking for a new assignment at work. Write down all the excuses and problems you came up with to reject the idea. For example, perhaps you didn't ask for the new assignment because you'd never done anything similar before, didn't know if you could handle the extra workload, and you weren't sure if it was already assigned to someone else.

- **Weigh each excuse for validity.** Take each item on the list and think through whether they are really obstacles that could block you from achieving your goals . . . or just excuses based on fear or procrastination. In the example above, not having enough experience could potentially keep you from getting the assignment. But fears about handling the extra workload or wondering if it has already gone to someone else will not prevent you from getting the assignment. Let's face it: They are simply excuses not to go for what you want.

- **Think of ways to overcome your obstacles.** So you don't quite have the experience to take on the project. How can you overcome this? Maybe you are willing to cooperate with a co-worker who *does* have the experience, so you can learn what you will need to know on this project and you can work independently the next time. Or maybe you can take on a smaller project until you build up to the one you want. If your dream assignment has indeed gone to someone else, try to develop a few main reasons why that person had the advantage over you. Perhaps there are areas for you to focus on going forward to improve your chances for the next opening.

- **Reclaim your dreams.** Once you have successfully broken down all your excuses, re-imagine the dream. You are the savvy team leader of the most important assignment for the company. You handle it with expertise and efficiency. Is it still a dream that fits? Are you still interested in being the team leader? If so, it's yours for the taking.

Turn It Around

"Work is either fun or drudgery. It depends on your attitude. I like fun."
—COLLEEN C. BARRETT,
president and COO of Southwest Airlines

Take a look at the following negative statements that we often hear from women who are filled with self-doubt. If you've ever found yourself making similar claims, make it a priority to banish that negativity from your mind because it can hold you back from success. Review the positive statements as inspiration on how to spin things to your advantage.

Negative: What others think of me is more important than what I think of myself.

Positive: I'm proud of my own values and definition of success, which help guide me in all I do.

Negative: I find myself apologizing, even when I've done nothing wrong.

Positive: Instead of constantly saying "I'm sorry," I'll listen and say "I understand."

Negative: I never forgive myself for mistakes.

Positive: I acknowledge my mistakes and learn from them. Mistakes are part of growing.

Negative: I bend over backwards to please other people rather than myself.

Positive: It's not up to me to make everyone happy. My happiness is important, too.

Negative: I never think I've done enough, or done it well enough.

Positive: I'm satisfied knowing that I did my very best. I work hard and deserve credit.

Negative: Deep down, I know I am not as good as other people.

Positive: I'm very good at what I do and have my own self-worth.

Negative: I'm afraid people will find out I am a fraud.

Positive: My successes are genuine. If I value them, I know others will value them, too.

If you think any of these negative thoughts often, be honest with yourself and try to determine why you are thinking them. Some things a book can't solve, but awareness of your feelings is key. If you find you can't turn these statements around, or you think negative thoughts too often, it may be time to seek help from a professional counselor.

Clear the Path to Success

A LESSON IN DETERMINATION

"You may be disappointed if you fail, but you are doomed if you do not try."
—BEVERLY SILLS

The main quality that differentiates successful people from the rest of the pack is sheer determination. They keep on going, no matter what, until they reach their goals. Yes, Virginia, they believe in themselves. They know full well that there are smarter, savvier, more talented people out there, but they also know that full-throttle motivation makes up for a lot. Attitude is key. Hard work beats talent when talent doesn't work hard.

 IT WORKS FOR ME ....

Step out of your comfort zone

"I was married for one week before I moved to New York from Trinidad. I arrived with only two suitcases. If I had lost one, there went half my possessions. I was a new graduate, new to marriage, and in a new country. To get ahead in your career, you have to be willing to take risks. Successful people have positive attitudes and tons of self-confidence. They're willing to take risks because they know that even if they mess up, they'll learn from the experience and can keep on going." —Donna Vieira, vice president, OPEN: The Small Business Network from American Express

Family and friends can detour your determination through their own negativity and doubt. Once you've committed to your goals, strengthen support from family and friends by communicating your plans and keeping them in the loop. As you learned earlier in this chapter, you set your *own* goals and define success on your own terms, not on the ideals of friends and family.

The biggest stumbling block to determination, of course, is fear of failure.

IT WORKS FOR ME

Dream big

Today show news anchor Ann Curry says, "Don't give up just because you are told no. We've all been told no, but we've never allowed it to stop us from pushing ahead. Katie Couric was told by executives at CNN that they never wanted to see her on-air again. Matt Lauer has been fired from more jobs than I can count on both hands. Al Roker has been told he has a face for radio. I was told there was no place for an Asian woman in broadcasting.

"When I was in my twenties, my brother died. My family wanted me to stay in Oregon, work at the sawmill, and live a nice safe life. I knew I had two choices: I could either live in fear or I could seize the day. I chose the latter. Once I made that decision, I have never looked back."

Often, women's fear of rejection, failure, and looking stupid or weak can stand in the way of their risk-taking and derail their determination. Keep in mind that rejection is not personal. It's usually just a disparity between what you're offering and what the other person wants at the time. Think of it as an actor might. No matter how talented you are, if you are short and blonde when the role demands tall and dark, you will not get that part. Develop a thick skin and move on.

According to life coach Rhonda Britten, in order to learn to take risks, you should focus on actions rather than feelings. Focus on building new skills. Britten suggests framing a problem in a way that acknowledges your feelings, but doesn't let them control you. For instance, complaining, "I can't get a job because of the economy" creates an excuse, a stopping point. A more positive approach that leads to action would be, "The economy is difficult right now and I'm afraid I'll have a hard time getting a job, so I think I need to take a class to improve my chances."

Talking out loud about a problem also helps diminish fear. We often tend to turn molehills into mountains in our minds. Vocalizing our concerns, even to just ourselves, cuts them down to size.

Failure is in the eye of the beholder: Think of it as feedback—a tool that teaches us how we can improve. The only real failure is the failure to try.

Roadblocks to Positive Thinking

"Even if you're on the right track, you'll get run over if you just sit there."
—WILL ROGERS

We all have our own stumbling blocks and hang-ups that prevent us from seeing ourselves in a successful position. Fear, procrastination, anxiety, and stress all prevent us from thinking positively. Don't let old thinking patterns ruin new dreams.

LOW SELF-ESTEEM

It's hard to think of yourself as successful when you have no confidence in any of your abilities. To lift your self-esteem:

- Focus on what you are good at and give yourself a break on the rest. For example, don't measure your value based on the fact that you're not the best at designing PowerPoint presentations. Instead, focus on what you do have to offer the team—top-notch speaking skills and a great sales record.

- Surround yourself with positives—positive friends, upbeat music, happy thoughts, and your favorite memories. Don't let your environment drag you down. Call your best pal and ask her to list her favorite things about you. Call a relative and ask him or her to remind you of how far you've come. Put on your favorite soundtrack, start dancing, and feel your energy return.

- Nobody's perfect. So stop expecting yourself to be perfect. Forgive yourself. Write down all the little things nagging on your mind that you have "done wrong" lately, and then put them in perspective. In five years, will they be that big of a deal? Probably not.

• Remember that you are not alone. You can turn to others for help and inspiration. From family and friends, to support groups, churches, temples, and other community resources, find someone who has been in your position before and can offer insight and a shoulder to lean on.

FEAR

It is okay to be afraid. It is not okay to let your fears control what you think and do. To get a handle on your fears:

• First, figure out what you're afraid of. Is it fear of running out of money? Fear of losing your stability? More than likely, what you're really afraid of is failure. Don't let a fear of failure prevent you from trying to succeed.

• Consider the journey. Understand that succeeding is not an end in itself, it's a process, a way to live your life, holding up your ideals and reaching to achieve them.

• Remember that failing is honorable, too. As long as you can pick yourself back up, as long as you learned something from the experience, failure is okay. Everyone fails at some point.

• Look at successful mentors and role models. Ask *why* they're role models and ask yourself why you chose them. Follow their fearless example.

• Examine your goals. Make sure that what you're aiming for is what you really want. Maybe your fears are trying to tell you something, that you are going down the wrong path, that you need to look before you leap. Don't sabotage yourself by pretending you want something you don't, or by ignoring your fears.

IT WORKS FOR ME

Charm your fears away

Purchase a charm bracelet and add a charm for each fear. A car for fear of driving, a megaphone for fear of public speaking, and a computer for fear of communicating. Wear it when you know you're going to be in a stressful situation, and let the charms serve as worry beads.

WAITING FOR PERMISSION

Another problem women have is waiting for permission to succeed. Women have been taught to be submissive for so many centuries that many of us think men, or even more powerful women, must give us a signal to succeed before we're able to move forward, to be positive, to think and speak for ourselves. It's time to say "bye-bye" to this stumbling block, as you see that you have the right—the obligation—to think, decide, and act for yourself. How? As you do the exercises in this chapter, you will begin to see that nobody can stand in your way unless you allow them to do so. It's up to you to grant yourself the permission to succeed.

Tools to Win

EXPECT TO SUCCEED

Make a wish list. Include every dream, every wish, every desire. Have you always wanted to fly first class? List it. Do five-star restaurants make you ravenous? Include them. Have you always dreamed of a job full of power, glamour, and five hundred people working under you? Write it down. Include the man of your dreams. A boat. A job in an exotic, far-off city. Defining your goals, your desires, is the first step in achieving them, so dream big, and dream positive. Nobody gets everything they want out of life, but you won't get anything if you don't identify it and go after it. This is your chance to face your daydreams and start the process of making them pay off.

BLOCK THE BAD VIBES

"Let go of being perfect. Perfect is for a fourth-grade spelling bee. Business is about making smart decisions, not about being perfect."

—GAIL EVANS,

former executive vice president of CNN News Group

Get rid of doubts and feelings of inferiority. They are the chains that hold you back from soaring. The best way to get rid of them is first to recognize them and then to banish them. Tell yourself you have as much right to success as anyone else in the world, and if you ever begin to doubt that, go back and read your journal. Read what's good about you and the great things other people have said about you. If you doubt your goals, not only will you never achieve them, you'll never even try.

Have you had failures? Who hasn't? Bad breaks, bad luck, unfaithful friends, disappointments big and small. It's on the ashes of your problems that you will build the foundations for your towers of success. Learn from them, put them in the past, and move on. If you're still standing and breathing, the worst failures haven't vanquished you. Take responsibility for your mistakes, but don't let them rule you. Analyze past failures to find out why you failed. Be honest with yourself, and don't blame others for your own mistakes. Look at the lesson in each mistake and learn it. If you failed in the past because you weren't organized enough, get organized for the next time.

Here's a short exercise to help erase any negative ideas about your dreams. Get out your journal, make four columns, and label them:

1. Benefits of not succeeding (can stay in my comfort zone)

2. Costs of not succeeding (remain unhappy at work, inability to learn new skills)

3. Benefits of succeeding (long-term happiness, financial independence)

4. Costs of succeeding (temporary feelings of instability, increased workload)

Give yourself a few minutes to assess the columns, then start writing. If the costs outweigh the benefits, it's time for a major attitude adjustment! Study the benefits and remind yourself of them daily.

As you grow and change in your professional life, take the time every now and again to reconsider your definition of success. What seems inspiring and positive today may be tomorrow's energy-draining career track. If you no longer think positively about your career, you don't have to stick with it. Of course you should finish what you start and give each position a fair shake, but don't keep going on a path you know is wrong. Being a floor nurse may have been great when you had all the energy in the world and just graduated from college, but does it fit who you are now? There is no beginning or end to positive thinking. It is a skill that should be applied continuously throughout your life—both personally and professionally. A positive attitude and great optimism are also the foundations for successful goal setting, which is discussed in the next chapter on your road to advancement.

CHAPTER TWO

Go for the Goal
Proper Planning Will Get You There

"You can't build a reputation on what you intend to do."

—LIZ SMITH,
legendary gossip columnist

We live in a world with an incredible amount of choices—from the mundane *(What shade of lipstick should I wear? Should my diet be low-fat or low-carb?)* to the profound *(Where do I want to live? Where will I work? When should I start a family?)*. With all the brands, options, and information available to us, it can be overwhelming. Setting goals helps us sort it all out.

Women set goals every day and stick to them tenaciously. Have you ever stared in disbelief at the friend who has all her holiday shopping done by August? Or the cancer survivor who completes a 5k run? Yet when it comes to our careers, many of us don't do a whole lot of planning. We start out looking for the job we want, but end up taking what we can get. We may luck into something that we love, but more often than not, we settle for work, not our "life's work." Considering the amount of time we spend on the job, we're not really making the connection between our careers and our happiness, passion, or fulfillment. It doesn't have to be that way.

Setting goals gives you the long-term vision of where you want to go in life, and the short-term steps to get there. With all the roles that we as women juggle in our lives, careful thought and planning in our careers is especially essential. With the right plan, detours—starting a family, caring for elderly parents, relocating to be with a partner—become part of the journey, rather than a disruption.

Setting goals is about making choices. We're going to show you, step by step, how to put passion and planning into finding a realistic and satisfying career goal. But, to get what you want, you have to know what you want.

Setting Your Goal

DREAM ON

There are even more careers and industries than there are entrées on a diner menu. So many choices, but you can only pick one at a time. You have to pick something off the menu of careers that most closely suits who you are and what will make you happy.

Personally, we want the grilled cheese sandwich. A cure for cancer. Some new diamond earrings and that ever-elusive perfect shade of red lipstick. These things are easy to want because they don't require much thinking. We simply want them. We didn't take money into consideration, or what our friends would say, or the latest health and nutrition study. We aren't thinking about reality, just about what we want.

Ignore reality for a moment. This is the first step toward finding out what you want. For just a moment, don't become bogged down with the details or the problems with your ideas. Free your imagination from all the "ifs," "ands," and "buts" of life. Dust off those forgotten childhood dreams and look for clues as to how you really see yourself.

Maybe you want to be a singer. Maybe you want to work from home, or write a book, or become a computer programmer, even though you are currently an elementary school teacher. What you want may not take a specific shape yet.

Claire Shipman, an award-winning broadcast journalist at ABC News, says *Dead Souls* by Nikolai Gogol might seem an unusual pick for her favorite book, "but that novel, and his literature in particular, are what inspired me to head off on my original journey to Russia, which in turn enabled me to launch a TV reporting career I never thought I'd have. Gogol, who is a terrifically dry and funny sort, was a master at highlighting the absurdities of Russian life, and life in general. He not only made me want to explore that strange and hysterically funny land from end to end, but also to find a way to tell vivid and finely drawn stories about people and lives myself."

Ask yourself what you would be doing if you didn't have to think about money. Look for broad ideas that you think would give meaning to your life. What would rock your world and make getting out of bed every morning worthwhile? Do you like helping people? Love to share your insights or experiences with others? Do you feel energized by challenges that are physical, intellectual, or emotional?

Look at your life as if you were near the end of it. How do you want to be remembered? Are there any regrets you think you'll have for things left undone or untried? This exercise will help you focus on the big picture, the stuff that is truly meaningful to you.

To put a puzzle together, you need all the pieces. Knowing what you want is not about putting the puzzle together; it is about finding the pieces. Once you have the pieces, you can set your career goal. In chapter 1, you learned how to think positively and define success on your own terms. The exercises in this chapter will help you find a career path that fits that definition.

GET REAL

Now that you've rediscovered old passions, it's time to get real. Is there a reason your dreams *can't* become a reality? You've thought of turning your love of white-water rafting into a career as an adventure guide, but when it comes down to it, you'd really rather stay dry on a daily basis. Or you're land-locked, and moving near the rapids just isn't an option. Brutal honesty is necessary here.

Sometimes there *is* a valid reason to set aside certain dreams and goals. Dreaming of becoming a ballerina after seeing a production of the *Nutcracker* when you were six is one thing, but if you're now twenty-six and have never taken a dance class, it's probably not the kind of dream on which to build your career goals. But being realistic doesn't mean being pessimistic. Don't let doomsday predictions keep you from trying, and don't try to tailor your dreams to the naysayers. If something gets you excited and enthused, even if it isn't easy, even if others try to discourage you, remember, just exploring the possibilities may lead you to finding your true niche. Maybe you can't be a ballerina, but that certainly doesn't stop you from pursuing a career in the arts. With a passion for ballet perhaps you're well suited for a position in administration at a performing arts center or within a company that manufactures or sells tutus.

PITFALLS TO PONDER

Where are you going?

"I knew I wanted to be in sports but I wasn't sure exactly where or how. I applied for hundreds of jobs, interned for a variety of sports properties, volunteered for the U.S. Olympic Festival, Amateur Athletic Foundation, and NCAA. I did anything and everything to keep my foot in the door. The only problem was I didn't know what kind of job I was looking for, nor did I understand what I was qualified for. Consequently, I spent a number of years moving in a lot of different directions. Some days I wanted to be a sports agent, other days I wanted to work in sports marketing for a professional team. I wasted a lot of time and went in a lot of different directions that could have been avoided had I gotten help. If you don't have a clearly defined path, recognize that and get help." —Becky Heidesch, CEO, Women's Sports Services, womensportsservices.com

Take stock of your personal values and your definition of success (from chapter 1). It may be crucial to you to make a lot of money, to have a socially responsible position, or to have an enduring effect on the world. Perhaps creative expression is your larger purpose in life. Your aims in these areas may not be mutually exclusive, but they can be in conflict. Know yourself, and how critical it will be for you to incorporate your ideals into your career goals.

Assess Yourself

This exercise will help you identify your strengths and weaknesses. Rate yourself on a scale of 1 (poor) to 5 (exceptional) on how skilled you are at each task. Keep in mind your experience level. You may have great sales skills for an entry-level professional, but poor skills for a manager. Be completely honest with yourself. It does you no good to gloss things over or deny your weaknesses.

_____ Negotiation

_____ Influencing skills

_____ Money management

_____ Customer service

_____ Dependability

_____ Presentation skills

_____ Marketing

_____ Enthusiasm

_____ General management skills

_____ Oral communication

_____ Written communication

_____ Interpersonal skills

_____ Creativity

_____ Time management

_____ Work ethic

_____ Dedication

_____ Crisis and stress management

_____ Family support

_____ Dealing with rejection
and failure

_____ Independence and autonomy

_____ Team work skills

_____ Leadership skills

_____ Listening skills   _____ Problem solving

_____ Computer skills   _____ Relevant work history

_____ Office etiquette

In addition to this list of general business skills, make another list of your specific job responsibilities, such as "preparing company taxes" or "developing client relationships."

Look at the items on the list that you marked as a 1, 2, or 3. These are the areas in which you need improvement. Items marked 4 or 5 are your personal strengths, which you should build your career around. Make two separate lists, one with your strengths and one with your "developmental areas."

Now look at your strengths and ask yourself:

- Does my current position utilize my biggest strengths? If not, what can I do to change that?

- Do I have strengths I hadn't considered before? How can I incorporate them into a career?

- Which of my strengths are the most marketable? Which would I consider a career in?

Take a look at your list of "development areas" and ask yourself:

- What are the biggest areas I can improve on in my current position? What effect are they having on my career and how can I compensate?

- What classes or workshops can I take to develop or increase skills in these areas?

- What behaviors might impede my career growth and how can I fix or eliminate them?

QUESTIONS TO ASK YOURSELF

- How do you rate your social skills? Do you get along well with people, or do interoffice politics turn you off?

- What level of stress or uncertainty can you live with?

- Did you get a general or specialized education, and have you used the knowledge gained in your work to date? Would you benefit from further study in the field, or have you discovered new interests that you'd like to pursue?

- Do you envision yourself with more or less responsibility? Are you a good manager? Creative? Or do you need a rigid schedule in order to get things done?

- Do you work well on your own, or are you more comfortable with thorough training and someone to guide you? Are you an idealist or a realist? An organizer or procrastinator?

OTHER THINGS TO CONSIDER

It's not only your skills and experiences that determine what you should set as a realistic career goal. Life's circumstances play a large role in what will work for you career-wise.

- What stage of life are you at? If you are responsible only for yourself, it might be the right time to take a big risk in pursuing your career goals. If you have family obligations, a mortgage, or have racked up huge credit card debt, that will, of course, need to be part of your consideration.

- Will "having it all" mean you'll be doing it all? Is there a family support system in place that will enable you to make the changes you'd like?

- Do you have the money for continued education, or to weather a

salary loss? Do you need more flexibility in your schedule to accommodate your family?

- How important are benefits? Insurance? Paid vacation? Matching
401(k) programs?

- What are your needs in terms of time, money, self-fulfillment?
What trade-offs will you have to make, and will you be able to
make, to achieve your goals?

If this seems like "Twenty Questions," it's not. It's way more than
that. But in order to map out your career path, you have to know where
the starting line is.

EVALUATE

You've now rediscovered your true passions and tempered those with a
realistic assessment of who you are and what you want. How does what
you've discovered translate to a dream job? Are you a math whiz with a
secret yen for stardom? Trading your banker's hours for a finance position
in the entertainment industry or with a nonprofit theatre organization
may be just the ticket.

Set the right goals for yourself. What are the patterns that have
emerged from your soul-searching? Distill what you've learned about
your strengths and desires into two or three specific fields that seem to
mesh.

It may be that you'll be looking at a radical career change. It's also
possible that what you really want are new challenges in your current
field: added responsibility, higher income, a higher level of management,
or a lateral move to gain new skills in a related area.

Perhaps your highest priority is more flexibility: more time off to
spend with your family or working for a political campaign, developing
an outside hobby or doing volunteer work. Your current job might become a "dream" job if you could cut your commute by working from
home part of the time. Separate your particular job from the general industry to see if it's the right choice but the wrong environment. In other

words, do you need to switch fields or just change companies? Should you perhaps start your own business, or give freelancing a try?

Compare the new fields you're considering to your past experience. Would the differences make the switch worthwhile? Would the similarities make a transition smoother? Are the things you liked or disliked about your previous jobs likely to occur again?

Pulling It All Together

This goal-setting exercise will help you organize all of your thoughts and ideas about what you truly want from a career, and help you pin down a career path that fits your needs.

1. Write down what you want to achieve by setting a new goal. What is the problem? Why are you seeking something new? (Is it money, time, a desire to work from home or start a family?)

2. List the aspects of your previous experiences that you liked and disliked. Use verbs and be action-focused. (For instance, Liked creating marketing plans. Hated conducting interviews.) Make two columns, or go back and see what you've written from the "Assess Yourself" section on pages 19 and 20. Write down things you've never done before but think you'd like to try in a new career.

3. Think of several careers or industries you would like to work in if you could pick anything you wanted. (Pharmaceutical sales? Grant writing?) List the responsibilities you perceive each of these positions to have, and what skills, education, or experience someone in this position would need.

4. Compare each of the potential positions and their responsibilities you outlined in #3 with the list of your likes and dislikes from #2. Do the job responsibilities match up? Will each possibility answer the needs you listed in #1?

5. Consider whether you have any relevant experience for any of these positions. If not, don't despair. This new career may take a little more work to achieve, but in the long run it'll be worth it because you're likely to be happier. Narrow it down to one career path that seems to strike the right chord.

You have just established your long-term career goal. It is the destination of where you want to be. Knowing where you're going is half the battle.

TRYING IT ON FOR SIZE

Before you cling to your goal too tightly, make sure it is the right fit. You may think you know everything you need to know, but your perception of a profession or even a specific company may be completely off base from what it is really like. You may think you want an accounting position in a Fortune 500 company, but when you realize how much bureaucracy you're likely to face, you may wish you'd stuck with a small, privately-owned business. Once you've set your goal, it is time to try it on for size, to do some research, and to make sure it really fits your definition of career success.

- **Gather as much information as possible.** A good place to start is by researching industries, companies, positions, and salaries to see if they fit your expectations. It's hard to predict the future, of course, but is your chosen industry expected to grow in the coming years? Given a seesawing economy, will there be a demand for the field in bad times as well as good?

- **Schedule an informational interview.** Someone who already has your desired job can offer a wealth of information. Does the reality match the ideal? Ask what their job responsibilities are, their likes and dislikes. A career in broadcasting may seem glamorous, but the competitiveness behind the scenes can be a real turn-off to some. Likewise, teaching in a classroom is a laudable goal, but are you prepared for the discipline problems that go with it? Make sure the position is really what you think it is. Once you have done your research, you can proceed with confidence.

● **Consider relocation.** While lawyers seem to be everywhere, aerospace engineers will find that major employers are based in a few specific locations. Research potential cities where you may end up living; explore the housing, schools, weather, and general quality of life to determine if they are acceptable to you. Plan a visit, if possible, to get a feel for the place.

● **Create a financial plan.** Determine if you'll need to work while pursuing your options, or if you have enough financial resources to live on while you transition.

Put Your Plan into Action

MAPPING OUT YOUR GOAL

Now that you've defined what your long-term career goal is, it's time to put the puzzle pieces together. How will you achieve your goals? What are the exact steps you need to take to reach your dreams?

Long-term goals are the big picture. Start with these and work backward. Don't imagine you'll be able to make just one big leap to get there. It's a cliché, but a journey of a thousand miles really does begin with a single step. Breaking your main goal down into bite-size pieces will make your task less overwhelming and more surmountable. The steps taken to reach long-term goals are short-term goals.

This exercise will help you define and set the short-term goals to reach your long-term career goals. Identify obstacles and set a deadline for each short-term goal.

1. Write your long-term goal in specific terms. "I want a career in public relations" is too vague. Instead, try "I want a career as an event planner in a small public relations boutique." This is the long-term goal you set in the exercise "Pulling It All Together," on page 23.

2. Figure out the steps to achieve this goal. Do you need to take any courses or acquire any new skills? Do you need to gain more experience through internships or freelance work? Do you need to set up an informational interview to find out more about how to proceed? These are your short-term goals.

3. Put your short-term goals in order. Find a starting point. What needs to come first? You can't secure an internship before you take a course to gain the required skills.

4. Now take each short-term goal and write out the specific steps of achieving each one. For example, if your short-term goal is to take a course, first you need to research schools or workshops, and then you need to sign up or apply for one. If your goal is to get an internship, first you need to write a résumé, then send it out to companies. Set a deadline for each goal: "I will have successfully taken the computer course by November."

5. As time goes by, monitor your progress. You may decide your goal is too ambitious or not ambitious enough. Simply revise your long-term and short-term goals, review what you have accomplished so far, and change paths. Example: Your original goal of becoming a psychologist must be put on hold because you simply aren't getting the grades you need to get into the right study program, let alone the required field work. You can revise your goal and apply your education to becoming a social worker or nurse in a psychiatric hospital.

 IT WORKS FOR ME ···

Do What Feels Right

While in journalism school at the University of Colorado, Michael Gelman received a lot of advice from his professors. Most of them said if he wanted a career in television, he'd have to start in a small market and hope to work his way up. He let it all sink in—and then abandoned their directives.

Instead, armed with an abundance of creativity and energy, Gelman headed to the Big Apple as an intern on an early version of what ultimately became *Live!,* the popular talk show now hosted by Regis Philbin and Kelly Ripa. He knew that "someone had to get those TV jobs, so why not me? I realized that these were ordinary people— nothing to put on a pedestal—and if they could do it, so could I."

That passion, guts, and logic worked: In 1987, after freelance assignments and staff stints, Gelman became the youngest execu- tive producer of a national talk show, and proceeded to turn the pro- gram into a ratings powerhouse.

Don't forget to include in your plan how you will overcome the prob- lems you expect to encounter, for instance, finding childcare so you can devote some time to your career or continue your education at night. Now is the time to get your support systems in place.

STAYING ON TRACK

Remember, first of all, that nothing is written in stone. Your roadmap's in hand, but not every career path is straight and narrow. Don't be dis- couraged by detours along the way. If we think of choosing a career path as more of a journey than a race, we don't have to be so daunted by it. People come to success from many different directions.

Career plans evolve and change as your life, interests, and opportuni- ties change. Allowing yourself to stay flexible means you can take advan- tage of swings in the economy, as well as new opportunities that may come your way. Recognize that there are times when your need, for ex- ample, to have health benefits may overshadow your goal to make a ca- reer switch, and don't get discouraged.

Keep your perspective. Many job searches take several months if not longer, so it makes sense to incorporate the possibility of interim jobs into your plans. If taking a part-time job becomes one of your short-term goals, don't look at it as a derailment from your long-range ideal. You may even find work that gives you a glimpse into the field you're aiming for, such as an office assistant for a homebuilder when you hope to pursue real estate sales.

As you achieve each short-term goal, fine-tune the next step. Have you learned anything new that might lead you to change your overall plan? Are you satisfied that your goals are still challenging, while not being impossible to reach?

That said, as you begin moving forward, keep the following tips in mind:

- **Prioritize your goals.** Stay focused on the most important ones to avoid feeling overwhelmed by too many goals.

- **Keep your goals small and achievable.** Reward yourself each step of the way as you complete them.

- **Goals should be positive.** Focus on what you do want to do, not what you don't want to do. Your goals should be specific, delineating exactly what action you are going to take.

- **Set goals you can control.** Going for rewards such as praise and recognition can lead to frustration. Instead, focus on goals that depend on your performance, such as a raise, bonus, or promotion for a job well done.

- **Take a break and rejuvenate.** You have the right to take care of yourself, and a little R&R can ward off major burnout. After all, the main goal behind all our goal-setting is to live life to the fullest.

In your quest to set and achieve goals, consider assembling your own personal board of directors. Just as large companies have boards to help with key decisions on their strategic direction, you should have four to six trusted individuals to turn to for solid advice and candid feedback on your career moves. This ranges from your thoughts on what to pursue and how to pursue it to monitoring your success and preventing you from veering off track. Throughout this book we'll talk about identifying and building a support system, and we highly encourage you to select your board of directors—and solicit their feedback—along the way.

*   *   *

Reflect on the goals you've identified and commit to making them a reality. Whether you're changing direction or forging ahead on a steady path, mapping out your journey will help make the destination more obtainable. In the next chapter we'll focus on positioning your assets to help fulfill your goals.

CHAPTER THREE

Repackage Your Assets
Apply Your Talents in a Whole New Way

"Each of us has a fire in our hearts for something.
It's our goal in life to find it and to keep it lit."

—MARY LOU RETTON, Olympic gymnast

The world around us is constantly in a state of reinvention. Just look at your toothpaste—it probably promises whiter, brighter teeth. Cars are safer and more luxurious with better fuel economy. Reinvention is another word for *change*. Women are always changing, whether it's our hair, clothing style, favorite haunts, even friendships and political attitudes.

But reinvention is not just change. Reinventing yourself means change with a twist, with a new face, a new outlook on life or career. Reinvention is the process by which you take everything you are and everything you've learned, and switch direction to head off on a new path. Sometimes it's a fork in your road: you stay in the same field, but in a new capacity, or you stay with your company but in a completely different role. Sometimes, however, you take a detour onto a brand-new highway by entering a totally new line of work.

Is It Time for Reinvention?

In this chapter you'll explore some of the scenarios and reasons for reinventing the direction of your career. You will learn how to marry your desires with various reinvention techniques and strategies to empower you to realize your goals. Sometimes you have to reinvent yourself to accommodate a fast-paced, ever-changing world. Sometimes, the need for change comes from within. Which of these apply to you?

- Your interests have changed.

- The market for your current skills has dried up.

- You've figured out your passion.

- You've discovered that your college major really isn't what you want to do.

- You've uncovered new talents you never knew you had.

- You're tired of the rut you're in.

- Your life's circumstances have changed.

- You have more time to devote to work.

- You need more money.

- You don't need the money.

- You need flexibility in your schedule.

- You want to be your own boss.

- You want to change the world.

 IT WORKS FOR ME ··

Passion is a key to change

Cynthia McKay was a successful attorney earning great money. Yet she was miserable. "I was seeking a change but terrified to leave a prestigious job that I had worked my life to acquire." All of that

changed overnight when McKay quit her job and opened a gift basket company. Today, LeGift.com is a profitable business with distri-
bution centers throughout the country. McKay's lessons:

- If you're unhappy where you work, make a change. You will likely
  make everyone else in your life miserable if you aren't content on
  the job.
- You'll always find naysayers who knock your goals as unrealistic.
  Don't allow opinions or negativity from others to stop you from
  accomplishing your dreams.
- If you have a passion that you think might work for you, go for it.
  Your passion is what will fuel your success.
- Sacrifices should be expected, but if you're happy, you'll be rewarded with a fulfilling career and the ability to enrich those
  around you.

You know all the ins and outs of your job and can figure out the answers before the questions even get asked. There's no place to go, no new
challenges awaiting you. What do you do? One solution: change companies or completely switch gears.

Look at Crystal. She was the office manager of a successful accounting
firm for fifteen years. She dealt with partners, clients, government officials, suppliers, and even cleaning crews. She hired and fired, wrote annual reviews, and had all the responsibility she could want. But there was
nowhere to advance, and after so many years, she didn't think she could
break out of the mold. Crystal was tired of it all. What could she ever do
but manage another accounting office?

After a hard look at her skills and accomplishments, Crystal realized
she'd accumulated all the attributes she needed to become a grant writer.
Her favorite aspects of her previous position were gathering facts, fig-
ures, and research; dealing with government officials; and writing annual
reviews. After careful research and a few classes, she began working with
a grant writer part-time to gain experience. Within a few years, she was
a successful grant writer in great demand, enjoying the challenges of a
new career.

Melody had spent years in sales. An excellent communicator, she was tired of the daily stress of making cold calls, and besides, her high-tech industry was in the doldrums. She decided to go back to school to learn a new field. While in school, she got involved in tutoring younger students and found she had a distinct talent for teaching. Switching gears, she earned a teacher's certificate and won a position on the college faculty.

Even though these two women have taken different paths, they share a common bond: both recognized a dullness to their days and boredom on their beats. They noticed a need for change and they embraced it. You can, too.

PITFALLS TO PONDER

Rethink your position before resigning it

"If what you are doing makes you miserable, you have to stop doing it or figure out a way to do it better. Women always say they can't keep quitting jobs, so you have to figure out some way to turn the job into a passion, find the challenge and figure out a way to embrace it. I believe you have to shift your focus and how you see it. You have to make it the right job. If your pattern is to constantly quit jobs, you need to look at yourself." —Gail Evans, author of *She Wins, You Win: A Guidebook for Making Women More Powerful* (Gotham Books, 2003).

Reinvention is not always a choice. Sometimes we're hit with a sledgehammer and we have to make a U-turn. Was your world suddenly flipped upside down? A baby can do that to you, but so can a heart attack or other illness—yours or someone close to you. You're widowed or divorced, the bottom fell out of your husband's job, and the bank account is awash in bright red. Your company phased out your job, a new boss brings in her pick to take your place, or your partner was transferred to a new city. Sometimes life forces you to assess your situation and begin to search for a new career.

Jamie was a successful personal shopper in a major city. Her husband, a physician, accepted a hospital post in a college town halfway across the country. Upon moving, Jamie realized there would be very little hope for her to succeed in her old job. Not only was there no major department store to link up with, the small community was mostly students—with notoriously empty pockets. Determined to make a career for herself, Jamie also wanted to meet people and become part of the community. She called on her resources, reviewed her skills, and found a position as a wedding planner with a local event planning boutique. As word of her work made its way through the neighboring towns, Jamie found herself with more jobs than she could handle.

IT WORKS FOR ME

You're never too old to reinvent yourself

Rhoda was sixty-three when her husband died of cancer. She'd looked forward to golden years of travel and ease, but her husband's protracted illness depleted the bulk of their retirement funds. She hadn't worked in decades, and she didn't think anyone would be willing to hire this "useless old hag," as she called herself. After visiting a counseling service, she thought about what she'd done with her life. She'd been president of more organizations than she could count. She'd run a volunteer soup kitchen, developed a shelter for homeless women with children, collected clothes and food, served on boards and held just about every office in every women's group in town. Writing it all down, she suddenly saw that she had quite an impressive résumé. Weighing her life skills and her likes and dislikes, she decided to go back to school in a two-year business administration program, then look for an office management position in a nonprofit agency.

Picking a Path

WHAT DO YOU LOVE AND HATE ABOUT YOUR CURRENT JOB?

We are all conditioned to think what we are doing now is the only thing we are suited for, but you are a multifaceted, multidimensional person, a unique being just crammed full of talents, skills, likes, and dislikes. Complete the personal assessments and goal-setting exercises in chapter 2 (pages 19–23) to determine what career path you'd like to take.

As you prepare to face the possibilities of the future, make a list of the things you love *and* hate about your current job. Hold on tight to this list, and pull it out whenever you're considering your next move. What you hate is as important as what you love, so avoid any job where those negative things are paramount. If you follow your passions, you can't help but be better off. Why do you want to reinvent yourself and what are you trying to leave behind?

ARE THERE OTHER INDUSTRIES YOU SHOULD CONSIDER?

When considering a new career path, especially when you're open to any number of options, a look at industries with expected growth can provide great insight. Similarly, you'll want to avoid those that are expected to become obsolete, especially if you have more than just a few career years ahead of you.

Fast-paced changes in technology rendered many careers obsolete in the last ten years, even though they experienced great booms for decades prior. It's rare that you meet a telex operator these days—her role was replaced by the popularity of the fax machine. And now email has led to the decreased usage of the fax. Many companies have cut back on live operators as voice recognition and touch-tone technology serves callers with cost-effective ease. The demand for airline reservation agents will ultimately decrease as travelers become more accustomed to the convenience and savings of booking online. A few of the fields where demand is expected to increase, especially for women:

Popular radio show host Cindy Simmons of top-rated Star 94 in Atlanta raves about *The Devil Wears Prada* (Doubleday, 2003), which is first-time novelist Lauren Weisberger's tale of the horrors and hilarity faced by an assistant to a top fashion magazine editor. "I only wish this book would have been around when I first got into radio, because it teaches three very important things about paying your dues: Never underestimate a good pair of comfortable shoes, no job is worth sacrificing your own being, and it can always be worse."

• **Law enforcement.** Women traditionally aren't drawn to positions where they're required to carry a gun, which means police forces are predominantly male. Now there's a major emphasis on behalf of local, state, and federal agencies to bring more women into the fold. Ambassador Frank Taylor of the U.S. Department of State, Bureau of Diplomatic Security, encourages women to become Special Agents. "I think the biggest misconception is that you have to be a six-foot-tall, 205-pound male to be an effective agent," he says. This is simply not true, since agents are trained to be effective regardless of their physical size. The second biggest misconception is that the profession is too dangerous. "There is an element of danger involved, but not as much as people usually think." Taylor is a strong advocate for encouraging women to consider this line of work. "Diversity is a critical tool for effective law enforcement. It is important to have members who reflect society. Our organization wants to look like America. We want to be a vibrant organization to reflect the country we serve."

• **Human resources.** According to Dan Black, campus recruiting leader at Ernst & Young, "Quality human resources professionals are more in demand today than ever. Competition is high because human resource professionals compete with people who are not even in their field. But in today's market, the majority of people will have to do a background check, even recent graduates, which has created a demand for more human resource professionals. Hiring the right candidate the first time is more important than ever."

• **Healthcare.** An aging population and longer life expectancy are two of the main reasons we're facing a critical nursing and healthcare services shortage. With fewer technicians to perform ultrasounds, X rays, and even mammograms, the public suffers with longer delays for routine care. For many positions, formal training can be obtained through time-efficient continuing education and certification programs.

- **Entertainment.** As Americans choose to spend more time at home for reasons of safety and comfort, opportunities in the arts and entertainment—from television production and moviemaking to creating music and promoting concerts—will stay strong. This extends to leisure activities close to home, meaning careers in sports, restaurant hospitality, and even exercise and healthy living will remain in demand.

- **Technology.** Just about all forms of engineering and the sciences—from electrical and mechanical engineers to quality assurance technicians and product development managers—will continue to generate solid paychecks with great advancement opportunity, especially for those candidates on the cutting edge.

WHERE CAN YOU FIND INFORMATION ON NEW CAREER AREAS?

If you know you want to leave your current career path, but aren't sure what you want to do, attend career fairs. Often, there are jobs out there you are qualified for that you didn't even know existed. Career fairs can introduce you to new ideas and companies you could work for. When you attend a career fair, dress in business attire and bring twenty to thirty copies of your résumé. Pick up as much literature as you can from different companies, and read job descriptions to see what interests you. If you think you've found a match, you already have the contact information of a company that is hiring! Tailor your résumé to fit that position and apply in the manner specified from the information you've gathered.

When you think you've found a career path you're interested in pursuing, join an association in that field. You will immediately immerse yourself in the new path and can decide whether or not it is truly for you as you assess your skills and abilities for your new profession. In addition, it looks great on a résumé and shows that you're genuinely committed to this field. And if you're a career changer with no prior experience in a specific field, this can help to demonstrate your desire to break into this new field.

Paving the Way

Once you have pinned down your new industry or career choice, you can begin packaging yourself to your new target market. You don't have to start over from scratch. What you've learned in one job can serve you well elsewhere, in ways you may not ever have considered. Instead of discounting your previous work history, look at it in a different light. Highlighting different aspects of your skills and experiences will give your work history the makeover it needs to attract employers in your new industry.

- **Learn everything you can about your new field.** Before you even consider your skills, you have to know what will be valued in your new career. Have you decided to go into human resources? Make a list of all the skills, experience, training, certification, or education human resources professionals should have. What is the job description of the position you are looking for? If you don't know what is essential in your new career path, ask a professional in that field. Look at positions in your field advertised in the classifieds or online job databases. What are the employers asking for? Conduct a search online for the title of your desired position, and you'll retrieve valuable information and resources.

- **Compare the essential job skills with your experience.** First take a look at your general skills, such as computer skills or communication skills. Many skills are widely transferable and valued in several industries. Dig a little. If you were an accountant and want to be a news reporter, your number crunching has given you great attention to detail and accuracy—two highly valued skills in journalism. Now think more about your specific experiences, such as organizations you belonged to, companies you worked for, and titles you held. They probably don't line up exactly with your new industry, but how have they prepared you? For example, your position as a social worker taught you how to handle disagreements and evaluate clients' well-being. Use specific experiences or anecdotes to illustrate how efficient you will be in customer service.

IT WORKS FOR ME

Matching your transferable skills

Brenda was a high school guidance counselor for fifteen years when she decided she wanted a little more glamour in her life. Though she enjoyed working with students, she wanted to become a personal assistant. After considering the skills a personal assistant must have, she identified a long list of transferable skills she'd gleaned from her guidance counselor position: flexibility, experience handling confidential information, listening and communicating skills, scheduling and daily planning, conflict resolution and problem solving, organization and filing. In an interview with a busy executive, she described her guidance counselor position as being a personal assistant to hundreds of teenagers. Not only did she organize their class schedules, she also set them up with scholarship and college information, counseled them through hard times, attended their school activities, and mediated conversations with their teachers and families. The executive was impressed with her dedication to her students and offered her the position.

With all the information you gathered from your self-assessments, tweak your résumé to include your transferable skills. When switching careers, it is often beneficial to use a functional résumé format, rather than the traditional chronological style. A functional résumé focuses on specific skills, not necessarily based on a progression of specific jobs you've held. A chronological résumé includes a rundown of your employment history starting with the most recent position. In either version, you'll want to include your previous experiences, but with a twist: Rewrite your résumé with an emphasis on your new career goal. The most important point here is to make potential employers see the you that you want to be, not the you that you used to be.

Make sure your personal appearance matches the new you. If your look needs repackaging too, start early, so all your face-to-face contacts see the new you. If you were a sales clerk in a funky retail boutique, and you're going into corporate life, check out what women are wearing in the boardroom before showing up in a miniskirt and fishnet hose.

With your goals set and your résumé in hand, you also have to determine how you're going to make the leap.

- **Try to make an internal transfer.** If your ideal job is right under your nose, build your skills and network effectively to make a transition right in your company. This kind of reinvention has the advantage of comfort level: You already know the people, they know you, and you probably won't lose benefits or seniority. The key here is to ask—to find out what's available and what you have to know to get it. Large companies sometimes offer an intranet of available internal opportunities.

- **Attend job fairs.** If you are taking a plunge into a completely different career, chances are you don't know a lot of contacts in that field. Job fairs can provide a great opportunity to network and meet people in your new industry.

- **Volunteer.** Forget the old maxim about never giving it away for free. Your talents and skills are your strongest selling point, and strategic sampling is a wonderful way to let people know about you. If you're starting a career as a fund-raiser, offer your services to local schools and charities. If you want to work for an art gallery, work with local restaurants and lounges and offer to coordinate art shows with paintings from local artists.

- **Ease yourself into a new career.** If you're a nurse but you want to be in sales, take a part-time job as a salesperson. Don't burn yourself out, but try a taste of what seems like the ideal job before abandoning a sure thing.

- **Go for it!** If you're at your wits' end, be prepared to quit and jump cold turkey into a new career. But don't expect instant success, tons of money, or a quick ride to the top. This is often the least effective way to make a successful transition, unless you have financial security or something lined up.

- **Network.** Let your network know that you are looking for a new position. Explain what field you are looking for, and why you've decided to make the leap. If you're launching a new career, hold an "expert" party to introduce yourself to those who can help you. If you're looking for a position as a paralegal, invite your cousin whose wife is a lawyer to a family barbeque. If you just got your massage therapy license, invite salon managers, gym trainers, or facialists who work in spas.

 IT WORKS FOR ME

Unpaid work yields valuable skills

"I found myself a victim of the technology bust and the downward spiral of the economy when my company eliminated my position along with four hundred others. In plotting my next move, I began writing out my strengths and everything that I'd done, regardless of whether it was voluntary or for pay. My exercise of self-discovery brought clarity and focus to my job search, and gave me a resurgence in self-confidence. It was amazing how much I had done and how much I knew. By drawing on things that I would not have ordinarily thought of as 'work experience,' such as extensive volunteer initiatives through my church, I was able to unearth a new skill set and potential career path that lie dormant inside me. When faced with the ability to start over or pursue something new, go back through previous jobs and look for valuable skills and abilities that you may have utilized and not realized." —Jabaria Willis, Washington, D.C.

RETURNING TO THE WORK FORCE

For many of us, career fell by the wayside as we took time off for child-rearing or the demands of our spouse's career. For these women, there are special concerns in reentering the job market.

If you were smart, you kept your skills and contacts up while you were out of the job market. If that eluded you, you still developed and maintained many transferable skills. You'll need to package them in a way that shows you are ready, willing, and qualified to handle anything that comes your way.

- **You managed a household budget.** That translates to fiscal responsibility, financial planning, and reconciliation.

- **You raised three kids.** Interpersonal skills, problem solving, decision-making, and supervision are a few of the skills you've perfected.

- **You were a team or class mother.** Think about the scheduling, organizing events, transportation, parties, and fund-raising. Team mothers should be considered for sainthood, or at least leadership positions.

- **You ran the book fair for your children's school.** Or maybe you volunteered to run the lunchroom, science fair, or a field day. Every skill you used for those tasks translates into a marketable job asset. Don't sell yourself short just because you gave away your talents. Every task you did can translate into skill-talk potential employers can understand. Setting goals, solving problems, providing support, and delegating are all transferable skills.

- **You were president of a charitable organization.** That deserves at least a few positive lines on your résumé. Think about everything you did from juggling schedules to motivating volunteers to meeting quotas and deadlines. You had to be a salesperson to get others involved and contributing. You had to soothe feelings and deal with disparate personalities. You had to try to please everybody, which is fabulous experience for reentering the work-for-pay world.

- **You chaired a committee.** You delegated, steered, implemented, set and achieved goals, and hustled.

See how it works?

You may want to consider easing yourself back into the market. One really easy way is through temping—taking temporary jobs at a variety of companies in a range of capacities, many of which have the possibility to turn into permanent positions. This does two things. It gets you acclimated without a major commitment, and it allows you to sample the climate and get a taste of different environments and different positions, before you're forced to decide what it is you want to do. Not only does the company get to "try before they buy," so do you. (We'll talk more about this later in the chapter.)

Another thing you'll want to do when reentering the workforce is build your confidence. Reading, talking to others, listening, and learning what's happening in the world of work will help. But the most important thing is to believe in yourself and believe that what you have to offer is valuable to an employer. Whatever you've been doing with your life has given you valuable experience and skills, and now you are ready to share them with the world.

Going It Alone

Women are starting businesses in record numbers, which can reap great rewards. The Small Business Association predicts that there will be about 10.7 million self-employed women by 2005, which is an increase of 77 percent since 1983. If you're considering going into business for yourself, there are many things to keep in mind since it takes sound planning and self-evaluation, as well as a thorough understanding of your anticipated product or service to succeed in this ever-more-competitive environment.

- **Expertise.** Do you know everything about your chosen field, or are you willing to invest the time to learn?

- **Financing.** Can you afford not to be earning any money while you get your business off the ground? Do you understand enough about money to be able to put together a credible financial plan? Can you afford to lose whatever investment you make if things don't go as planned?

- **Support.** Do you have a network of advisers, financial backers, and friends to help get you through the rough spots?

- **Uniqueness.** Is there a niche or a market for whatever it is you are choosing to do? You must research this before making any decision. You must find the hook—that thing that will make people flock to you instead of to the guy next door.

- **Time.** Are you willing to be invested in your business twenty-four hours a day, seven days a week? Are you willing to eat, drink, breathe, and sleep your business? Are those close to you willing to make that sacrifice as well?

- **Courage.** Are you able to tough it out during the hard times and not lose faith in your eventual success?

- **Independence.** Are you comfortable making your own decisions and sticking with them or are you indecisive and always second-guessing yourself?

- **Confidence.** Do you have the ability to assess situations and make quick, good decisions?

- **Flexibility.** Can you spot an opportunity and react to it quickly?

Among the valuable resources to explore if you're considering venturing out on your own are the Small Business Administration (sba.gov) and the National Association of Women Business Owners (nawbo.org).

With smart planning and clear goals, anything is possible. Whether you reinvent yourself out of necessity or personal desires, whether you switch positions, careers, or become an entrepreneur, strive to be the very best version of you.

CHAPTER FOUR

Create the Perfect Package
Maximize Your Strengths and
Minimize Your Weaknesses

"My drive in life is from a fear of being mediocre."

— MADONNA

In setting your goals, you assessed your skills and analyzed your deficiencies. Now that you know what you have to offer, and where you're going, you can build upon your strengths and make accommodations for your weaknesses to become the perfect package and ideal candidate. We'll discuss ways to add to your skill set so that you're better positioned for advancement.

Imagine you could read the mind of your boss or the person interviewing you. You would be able to say exactly what he or she wanted to hear. If you made a mistake, or left the wrong impression, you would be able to correct it immediately. You could quickly transform yourself into "the perfect package." We haven't yet learned how to read minds, but we can give you insight into what employers are looking for, and what their idea of the perfect candidate looks like.

Build Your Basic Skills

You can be successful even if you don't have *every* skill listed in a job description. However, some are more essential and better indicators of success than others.

- **Great interpersonal skills.** Strong interpersonal skills allow you to work with all personality types and enable you to communicate with co-workers and clients to achieve mutual goals. Employers want to know that you'll be a team player.

- **Leadership skills.** If you ever want to be a manager of people, you must learn to be an effective leader. Others will look to you for direction and motivation and you must be able to handle that responsibility. Managers want to see evidence that you have sought leadership roles and succeeded in them.

- **Willingness to sacrifice.** Nobody said success was easy. Sometimes you can't have it all. Be willing to put in long hours, extended travel, and the hard work required in your field when necessary. Keep it all in perspective, but showing that you will go the extra mile for your employer can lead to success.

- **Organizational skills.** It's crucial to know where things are and how to maximize resources. Be on top of what is going on, when deadlines are, and who is doing what. The ability to create systems that make information and documents available at your fingertips is a plus for you *and* your boss.

- **Experience.** No one starts at the top. Get experience any way you can, and give your all from your very first position. Use the experience you get to build your skills and work your way forward.

- **Intelligence and common sense.** Common sense helps you avoid problems and intelligence helps you solve them. You don't have to be a rocket scientist to be successful, but these traits are important in making sound decisions.

- **Positive attitude.** As we discussed earlier, successful people know how to keep their chins up and try again. They don't have a defeated attitude that prevents them from moving forward. They can handle criticism and learn from mistakes. They're pleasant to work with and motivate their co-workers.

ACQUIRING THE SKILLS YOU NEED

So how can you get these skills if you don't already have them? How can you demonstrate them to your current or potential employer? If you are lacking in skills there are numerous ways to make up for it.

- **Establish goals that help you overcome weaknesses.** For example, if English is your second language and you aren't completely comfortable with your proficiency, enroll in a course to improve that important skill. Some skills may take a matter of weeks to acquire; others will come through years of hard work and practice.

- **Volunteer.** Volunteering can give you a broad range of skills and experience. Decide what you want to improve on and then research companies or organizations you could volunteer for to learn new skills. Make sure you treat all volunteer positions seriously and dedicate the same time and energy you would to a paid position. Discuss with your new supervisor exactly what you want to gain from your experience.

- **Take a course.** Some skills, such as computer programming languages, are better learned through classes. Most communities offer short-term courses that meet once a week and can teach you a new computer program or skill. Look at local colleges, community centers, and organizations. It's possible your current employer will reimburse you for the cost of the class, so ask.

- **Become a member.** Joining a professional association is also a great way to gain new skills. There are associations for every profession imaginable, from executive assistants to mechanical engineers.

BOOK BREAK

Award-winning journalist Cokie Roberts, who covers politics for ABC News and provides analysis for National Public Radio, recommends *The Emperor's New Clothes*, the Hans Christian Andersen classic, to anyone interested in her line of work. She also suggests Louisa May Alcott's *Little Women*. "Doesn't everyone want to grow up to be Jo?" Roberts is also the author of the national bestseller *We Are Our Mother's Daughters* (William Morrow, 1998), which explores the diverse roles women have played throughout American history and the connections and distinctions among different generations.

Search online to find one with a chapter near you. It is not enough to join an association; to truly reap the benefits, you must be an active member. Go to meetings and conferences. Volunteer to work at events. Run for a leadership position as a way to gain new skills.

- **Learn from role models.** If the skill you wish to improve is more intangible, such as leadership qualities or team-building, seminars and workshops may be more effective. Look for lectures and guest speakers at colleges, community centers, and event facilities. You may also benefit from intensive self-help books, biographies of proven leaders, or even one-on-one coaching.

THE EXPERIENCE CONUNDRUM

Like it or not, to be the perfect job candidate, you must have experience. But how can you get that experience if no one will hire you? Whether you are switching careers, or just starting out, this can be a frustrating catch-22. The good news: There are several places you can find relevant experience outside the traditional workplace.

- Contact your alma mater and ask if they have job placement or career services for alumni. Often they will work with you to find a position or internship with local employers.

- Call a local business you would like to work for and offer to volunteer for a set period of time in exchange for a reference.

- Write a business proposal or idea for a company in the field you want to gain experience in, and submit it to employers until you find someone who will take you up on the project. (Just make sure you have done your research and are able to follow through.)

• Consider taking an assignment through the Peace Corps, or similar organizations. These positions are highly respected and offer great education and experience. World travel and cultural experiences can often compensate for specific education and experience.

You can also build experience from the position you're in. Even if your job is the bottom of the professional barrel, even if your title is "Manager of Grunt Work," you can still glean relevant experience. The key is to create it. Keep in mind your desired field and look for opportunities that can advance your career.

For example, if you are a receptionist who wants to be in journalism, ask if there are any documents you can edit or interview tapes you can transcribe. Once you have successfully done that for a few months, ask to write some assignments as well. If you are a waitress who wants to be in public relations, ask if you can write press releases and develop promotions to publicize the restaurant.

Most employers will be happy to give you a chance. They want the most amount of work done at the lowest cost. Make them an offer they can't refuse and you will gain valuable experience while rising to these new challenges.

 IT WORKS FOR ME ···

Ask questions, take initiative

"Early in my career I applied for an editor position in another division of my company. The interview went well, but I didn't get the job. That division was where I really wanted to work someday, so I approached the publisher and asked her if she'd be willing to give me some feedback about my interview. I asked what I needed to do to get a job in her division. She suggested some areas in which I needed additional experience and over the next few months I started working on filling those gaps. When another editor position opened, I applied again and got the job. The publisher said she

hired me because she was impressed that I had asked for some direction and taken the initiative to follow through with it." —Leslie
Banks, marketing director, Dearborn Trade Publishing

Mastering the Not-So-Basic Skills

FIRST IMPRESSIONS

Interviewers size you up from your very first contact, whether it is a
cover letter, email, or phone call. Throughout the entire process, they are
trying to weed out candidates, so it is important to make a positive first
impression—and keep on making one. There is no margin for error; you
must get it exactly right the first time. A UCLA psychologist conducted
a study that suggested our first impressions are based on 55 percent
visual information and 38 percent voice information; the remaining 7
percent is based on what we actually say. Dress nicely and make sure
your grooming is impeccable. If you're unsure, get a second opinion
about your appearance from someone you know, and a third from someone you don't know. In addition, keep your hand gestures to a minimum,
don't fidget, maintain eye contact, do not cross your arms, and try to lean
slightly forward with a straight, not hunched, back to show you are listening and interested.

Don't forget your first impression is often made by your résumé. It
must be free of grammatical and spelling mistakes, and must appear professional and intelligent.

RÉSUMÉS

Your résumé is your sales tool, written with a specific audience in mind
about a specific type of position. Your résumé should reflect how your
past has prepared you to fill the position you are aiming for. Don't apply
to seventeen job postings, says Donna Vieira, vice president, Line of
Credit and Loan, OPEN: The Small Business Network from American
Express. "We want to hire people who are focused—who want that
specific job, not just any job." With this in mind, here are a few strong

components to consider when evaluating the strengths of your current résumé. If you need basic formatting and style advice, our first book, *Women For Hire: The Ultimate Guide to Getting a Job*, goes into detail on this topic.

IT WORKS FOR ME

Online nouns are profound

CareerBuilder.com, a leader in online recruitment, suggests job-seekers describe their experience using nouns rather than the standard action-verb type résumé when applying online. Résumé scanners used by recruiters tend to search by nouns more often than verbs. Example: Instead of writing "managing projects," say "project manager."

- Start your résumé with a clear, specific objective that conveys two important points: who you are and what you are looking for. A weak objective is: "Experienced school psychologist." A strong objective is: "Results-focused, highly motivated educator with more than fifteen years of progressive and diverse experience in educational psychology, staff development, and administration."

- Use a chronological résumé format—one that lists your previous positions starting with the most recent—if you are staying in the same field. Use a functional format—one that highlights specific skills regardless of the time frame in which they were gained—if you are changing fields or just beginning your career at an unconventional time of life.

- If you are applying to many different types of jobs, write a different résumé tailored to each type of position. For example, a nurse might want to leverage her education and experience to move into pharmaceutical sales or she could pursue opportunities in healthcare administration. Two different versions of her résumé would emphasize prior accomplishments that relate best to those diverse goals.

- Instead of merely summarizing your *responsibilities* for each position, focus on translating your most impressive *accomplishments* in each role. Whenever possible, build your résumé bullets based on PARs statements, which cover Problem-Action-Results. Try to incorporate what the problem was, what action you took to solve it, and the results you achieved. For example: "Designed and implemented a comprehensive marketing campaign to revive weak sales, which resulted in increased revenue beyond the division's quota. Ranked highest sales manager throughout the country."

- If you have a vast amount of experience, remove any old jobs from your résumé that are irrelevant to the position you are applying for. If you are applying for a finance position and have held three consecutive finance positions, all with increasing responsibilities, you don't need to include the executive assistant position you held nine years ago.

- If you worked for the same company for more than a couple of years, in different roles, write out each title you held in succession. If you had the same title or position the entire time, show an increase of responsibilities. A potential employer will look for progression.

 IT WORKS FOR ME ·

Update online resumes often

"To avoid getting caught up in the Internet black hole, update your résumé every week on each website that it's posted on. Even if it's a small change, it will keep your résumé at the top of the pool," advises Melodi Ramirez, senior engineering recruiter, Aerotek. "When I'm searching for candidates on the Internet, the résumés are brought up by the date last revised. Therefore, if you posted your résumé online six months ago, don't count on me getting to it. Instead, I'll find a qualified candidate who has posted or updated their résumé within the last month or so."

A PROFESSIONAL PORTFOLIO—YOUR SUCCESS ACCESSORY

Consider a professional portfolio as another tool to help you land a job. Regardless of your field, a portfolio can help you track successes, display important documents such as your résumé, and help you categorize, store, and protect your successes in a written format. Your portfolio will help you articulate your qualifications and experience to employers.

To put together a professional portfolio, begin by making lists. Start by listing all your accomplishments, experience, and education, and gathering all the documents that you might want to include.

- **List your accomplishments.** Every day, or at least several times a week, write your successes. Write down all the major projects you are working on, and detail the steps you're taking to finish them. Did you create a database? Did you negotiate a deal that resulted in savings of $50,000? Maybe you secured a great new client, reorganized the filing system, or attended a networking event. No matter how little it seems, write it down. It doesn't have to be only accomplishments at work, either. If you've successfully rounded up a group of eight-year-old girls and taken them on a Girl Scout trip, write it down. List any positions you hold or committees you belong to, volunteer positions, any associations, any conferences you've attended, and any classes you've taken.

- **List the positive feedback you've received.** Jot down any compliments or comments you receive on your performance, no matter who they came from. Keep a record of the positive statements you get in reviews and personal evaluations. Save and print out emails. Keep thank-you notes, cards, and letters of recommendation in the journal as well. If applicable to your position, gather photos that illustrate your efforts. If you're an artist, gather examples of your work. If you're a writer, gather writing samples. If you are an event planner, take photos from your events.

- **List your skills.** Write down both comments about your performance such as, "I am great at balancing budgets," and comments about your personal skills as well, such as, "I have wonderful attention to detail skills."

By now, you should have compiled an extensive list of your professional accomplishments. Of course, you can't include them all. Like your résumé, the contents of your portfolio should be tailored to each employer. What you choose to show one employer may not impress the next employer, so review your portfolio before every interview. Buy a portfolio that catches your eye from the local bookstore and use it to display the highlights of your career. Your portfolio is a direct reflection of your work, so the content must be well-organized, well-edited, and enticing. Divide it into sections, such as résumé, letters of recommendation, samples, skills list, or any sections that would make sense for the position you are applying for. The contents of your portfolio should display a wide variety of your skills. List the skills you have for the position you are applying for, any education or classes you took to develop the skills, and quantifiable examples of how you performed the skill for past employers.

The format in which you present your portfolio depends on each person, scenario, and position. Consider whether it would be more appropriate to prepare an online portfolio, a leave-behind book, a CD, or another format. Your portfolio should reflect your creativity and ability to generate original ideas. Include a few great business ideas for your industry and the company you are interviewing for. Also important to incorporate are letters of recommendation; positive feedback from clients, coworkers, and supervisors; and glowing employee evaluations.

Be prepared to explain every item you include in the portfolio. Have stories and anecdotes ready to share. And bring your portfolio to every interview. Be prepared to leave it for further review if necessary.

 IT WORKS FOR ME ....

Portfolios as sales tools, not scrapbooks

Damian Bazadona, president of Situation Marketing, a web development and online advertising company, has hired many graphic artists and seen even more portfolios. "When you bring something to an interview, the physical layout and appearance are very important. It reflects how you would give a product or presentation to a customer. What is in a portfolio must be relevant to that specific company. Don't show billboard designs to a web-designing company, unless you are able to explain *why* you are showing it. Use the portfolio as a sales tool for yourself, not just a scrapbook. If you want to go above and beyond with your portfolio, have it available on a website, too. That way your interviewer can see it again or show it to a partner."

REFERENCES

References play an important part in the job search process. Don't ruin a good thing with bad references. They should help you seal the deal, not lose the offer. Have your references ready to go, so that when someone asks for them, you can hand them over.

- **Choose wisely.** Your references should be professionals, preferably in a position of authority or responsibility. Clients, former bosses, and colleagues all make fantastic references, as long as they are articulate, positive, reliable people.

- **Ask permission.** Don't provide someone's name as a reference without telling them. If they are put on the spot by an employer, they won't be prepared with glowing things to say about you. And, you never know how they may feel about you. Asking them permission gives them the opportunity to tell you they don't feel comfortable giving you a reference. But, if you don't give them the opportunity to decline, and they do have negative feelings about you, you don't want them speaking to a prospective employer!

- **Prep your references.** Run through a list of questions employers will probably ask and make sure their answers jive with your story. Give them a copy of your current résumé ahead of time, and tell them what you'd like them to say or highlight about your responsibilities. Explain what the position you are applying for entails. Make sure you know what they will say about your responsibilities. Explain what the position you are applying for entails. Make sure you know what they will say about you.

- **Bring letters of recommendation.** If you have unsolicited letters of praise from customers, co-workers, or supervisors, bring them along. Unsolicited praise is often the most convincing.

- **Leave it off your résumé.** Don't write "References available upon request" either. Employers know that if they ask for references, you will provide them.

INTERVIEWS

"In a competitive job market such as today's, it is essential to possess a high level of confidence and self-esteem. When interviewing for a position, you have to know you are the right person for the job."
—KAREN DONAHOE,
training supervisor, Southwest Airlines

The interview is your best shot at making a great impression, but just because they called you in doesn't mean you're any closer to an offer. Most employers review hundreds of résumés to find five to seven potential candidates for one position.

- **Consider the position.** Think about the responsibilities involved, required skills, level, and type of company. Know every detail and imagine the kinds of projects and duties you would be involved with. Ask a professional in a similar position what kinds of responsibilities they have and what would impress their employer.

- **Research the company.** Go beyond reading the website. Read trade journals and other industry magazines for any information you can find. Try to find their biggest clients, goals, and any new endeavors. Know their major competitors and trends in the field.

- **Consider your past experiences and skills.** What do you have to offer this particular company? What can you bring to the position?

Practice saying aloud what you can offer the company based on their needs and your relevant knowledge and experience.

• **Think outside of the box.** Go into the interview with a couple of strong business ideas you could implement if you were hired. This will help the employer "see" you in the position.

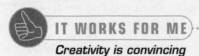

IT WORKS FOR ME

Creativity is convincing

"I once received a very unique Murano glass paperweight in the mail, along with a résumé and a very articulate cover letter from a woman seeking a top merchandising position. Her good taste stood out because of the paperweight. Being the merchant that I am, I admired the design and wanted to feature it in our catalog. I sourced it and our customers loved it. A strong résumé is always essential but a hands-on test is necessary to finalize my decision. The candidate for that merchandising position became our senior buyer and an incredible asset to our company. What it took was doing something unique like sending me a great product to know that the candidate had potential." —Lillian Vernon, founding chairman of Lillian Vernon Corporation

• **Identify any problem areas.** If you lack an element of experience for a position, be prepared to address that issue. How will you compensate? Explain that you are a quick study and are willing to take a course or put in extra hours on your own time to develop this area.

• **Practice answering common interview questions.** Remember, the heart of each question is really asking, "Why should I hire you?" Even simple, straightforward questions like, "Tell me about yourself," tend to trip people up.

A popular new trend is the use of **behavior-based questions** in an interview. Behavior-based questions focus on the idea that past performance is the best indicator of future performance. So rather than asking a hypothetical question, like, "What would you do to sell our product?" more companies are asking "What did you do to increase sales of your current employer's products?" Companies want to know what you did so that you can repeat that success to their advantage. Behavior-based questions include, "Describe a time when you were part of a team where there was conflict between members," or "Describe a time when you had to satisfy an unhappy customer."

Interviewers often asked behavior-based questions to solicit an unrehearsed, natural response. They know that asking the right questions is the key to getting the information they want, and they want to gather information about your behavior. Behavior-based questions give an interviewer insight into how you would act in certain situations, and the kind of decisions you might make.

One candidate we know interviewed for a sales position at an international overnight delivery company. A team of three interviewers handed her a pen and asked her to sell it to them because they wanted to test her sales style and method. Even though she was a seasoned sales pro, the candidate was so nervous and unprepared for an unexpected question that she couldn't think of what to say. She stumbled by touting the color and texture of the pen, instead of trying to spark a conversation to understand her potential buyers' needs, which is commonly thought of as the best initial sales approach. In the end, the interviewers didn't "buy" her sales pitch and, needless to say, she didn't get the job.

To prepare for behavior-based questions, brainstorm a list of anecdotes and examples of your past performance at work. Reread the responsibilities listed in the job description of the position you are applying for, and think of a few examples of when you demonstrated each skill in your previous jobs. Make a list of your hobbies, such as books you've read or clubs you belong to, especially any that relate to your field.

It is a well-known fact it is not always the best candidate who gets the job. Don't be passed over due to lack of preparation or the inability to articulate your skills and interest in the position.

Little details make the difference

Jerry Hocutt, who hosts Cold Calling for Cowards seminars, suggests using your body language to enhance your message.

- **Ace the handshake.** If it is dead-fish, you will seem weak, wimpy, and indecisive.
- **Be aware of your body language.** When sitting in a chair, sit up straight with your hands in sight. Try not to take a chair directly across from someone, as this is an adversarial position. If you must sit directly across from someone, angle your body.
- **Stand up.** Try to stand and do a presentation or go to a white board while your audience remains seated. This forces them to raise their chin at you and they will feel better about you. It is a sign of respect. It also gives you the platform to speak. This is why most speakers will stand or be elevated. You have a dominant position. When you sit, you give up the floor.

Another type of question you'll likely run into in an interview is the **puzzle question,** which tests a job-seeker's problem-solving skills and analytical thinking. William Poundstone, author of *How Would You Move Mount Fuji?* (Little, Brown & Company, 2003), says, "Puzzle interviews are very popular in consulting and technology. Technology is changing so quickly that it is not enough to hire someone based on technical skills and know-how. What they know now may be obsolete in a matter of years so employers are looking for candidates capable of learning new skills and creating new technology.

"Puzzles are designed to defeat typical intuition and logic. The first thought that pops into your head is probably wrong," Poundstone says. A good tactic for answering puzzle interview questions is to introduce your first idea with skepticism. This will fill the dead air and allow you time to think. Point out what is wrong with that answer. "Often, figuring out what doesn't work will lead you to what does."

Some companies might also pull pranks on the candidate. For example, an interviewer might pretend to be asleep at his desk when you walk in, just to see what you would do. The "correct" response is to leave a note on the desk with your number asking if he'd call you to reschedule the conversation when it is convenient for him.

The amount of puzzles you may be asked varies widely from company to company. Typically you could be asked one or two, but some companies such as Microsoft, Poundstone says, will ask up to two or three per interview in a series of five interviews a day for two days.

The best way to prepare is to practice solving puzzles. *How Would You Move Mount Fuji?* offers a list of questions commonly asked by Microsoft interviewers, as well as possible answers.

The Genius Is in the Details

It is not enough to have the skills and experience to excel in a position. Most employers expect you to have good industry knowledge and to keep up with industry trends. If you want to work overseas, you should know international business etiquette. If you want to work in journalism, read a daily newspaper and know your current events. Especially in fast-moving fields, you have to keep up through constant study, research, and even coursework.

- Read the newsletters you get from associations. They are full of tips, information, and upcoming events.

- Subscribe to a trade journal.

- Visit industry-related chat rooms or posting boards, often available on association websites. You can often trade ideas and ask for advice.

Here is an example of a real quiz used by a national news outlet to weed out applicants who claim they are interested in writing and producing but are not informed on even the most basic government affairs and current events. (Answers are at the end of the chapter.)

1. Briefly describe two major news stories found in today's newspaper.

2. What are the three branches of the U.S. government?

3. How many members serve in the U.S. Senate?

4. What is the difference between a bull market and a bear market?

5. What event triggered the 1992 riots in Los Angeles?

6. What U.S. president is known for his "midnight pardons"?

7. What is libel?

8. Who wrote *Uncle Tom's Cabin*?

9. On what continent is Iraq?

10. What is Napster?

As the quiz illustrates, having the skills and experience to perform a position is only the halfway mark. You need to go the extra mile and be well informed on your industry's trends and current events. So, if you're applying for a sports position, know team statistics and rankings. If you want a job in fashion, know who the top designers are, what their seasonal lines include, and who their target customers are.

Partner with a job-seeking friend and create your own industry-specific quizzes to see how you rate.

ARE YOU PROFESSIONALLY POLISHED?

Boston-based recruiter Patricia Levy, founder of Career Milestones, has devoted her career to interviewing candidates for top employers—from college students to senior executives. She evaluates the ideal woman based on her own top criteria to determine if she represents the perfect package.

Levy says first and foremost, the candidate must get it. "She sees the big picture, not just the job description." Candidates need to be proactive, she says, and match the needs of the client with potential solutions before the problem occurs. "She's a problem solver. She identifies a problem and suggests solutions. She has a sense of urgency and can prioritize and respond quickly when necessary."

Strong communication skills are also an important skill, Levy says. You must be able to articulate your thoughts clearly and concisely.

The best candidates are team players, respected by peers and co-workers. "A successful professional knows her strengths and weaknesses and has done a self-assessment. She is not afraid to develop her weaknesses and play on her strengths." Above all, be professional, both in and out of the office.

DO YOU NEED MORE EDUCATION?

For some career paths, the choice of whether or not to get an advanced degree is obvious. If you want to be a doctor, lawyer, or professor, the choice is clear. But what about the rest of us? What criteria should you use to make the decision to go back to school for an advanced degree? Graduate school demands time, money, emotional dedication, and can put family, friends, and personal life in a backseat. Sometimes the sacrifice can pay off. It can help you earn higher pay and secure better positions. A degree can be a great way to "create the perfect package." Weigh the decision carefully so you make the best choice for yourself.

What education will be necessary for the next step in your career? Some jobs may require a license or certification, others an advanced degree. Will having these make finding a job easier, or will you be considered overqualified for available positions?

Though you will invest money and time in graduate school, many new options for financial aid and distance learning are available. A recent report by the American Association of University Women (AAUW) Educational Foundation found that distance or online learning is on the rise, and women make up the majority of students. Sixty percent of non-traditional online learners are over twenty-five years old and female.

Swings in the economy make it hard to predict just how beneficial an MBA degree will be. A survey by *USA Today* of a top business school shows a drop from 90 percent to 55 percent in the number of graduates with job offers between the classes of 1998 and 2003. Yet according to the Graduate Management Admissions Council (GMAC), an association of graduate business schools, 67 percent of recent grads feel the value of their MBA is outstanding or excellent. According to GMAC, this may reflect a willingness of graduate students to view the MBA degree as a long-term investment in the future, rather than a quick fix.

It may be a good idea to gain work experience before getting an advanced degree. Many employers, for example, will look to hire MBAs who have interned within the company, or will first promote those who have industry experience. Take advantage of your company's tuition reimbursement policy, if there is one, and then network within your company to find an opportunity that will allow you to use your newfound skills for something you like—and to your employer's advantage!

IT WORKS FOR ME

Certification stamp of approval

Sally Kim, a technology specialist at Microsoft, recommends professional certification and training as an endorsement of your skills. Microsoft offers not only its employees, but all technology professionals, a variety of programs through its Certified Technical Education Centers (Microsoft.com/traincert/default.asp). The company also publishes *Microsoft Certified Professional Magazine* online at mcpmag.com/salarysurveys/, which tracks the advantages of certification such as salaries of certified versus uncertified professionals.

- **Think clearly about what you want out of an advanced degree.** What do you want it to do for your career? Are you looking to pick up specific skills? If you can't answer these questions, you need to do more research before pursuing higher education.

- **Be careful about pursuing an advanced degree in order to make a career change.** While it shows dedication to your new field, a master's degree may not be as valued as you would like it to be by employers. Internships, volunteer positions, and other work experience may be a quicker, cheaper, and more valuable tactic of switching careers, especially if you have a general undergraduate degree in a major such as business or communications.

- **Don't return to school just to buy time.** Many people fall into graduate school because they want to delay finding a job or they're afraid of rejection in the working world. Fear and laziness are not justified reasons for pursing an MBA.

- **Consider what field you want to study.** It may do you no good to obtain a master's degree in the same subject as your undergraduate degree. Instead, try to choose a degree that will add to your expertise, such as a business degree to complement a language degree, or a communications degree to offset a science degree.

- **Select the right school.** The first step is to research which schools are the highest ranked for your field of study. Then, apply to schools you think you can realistically get into. Consider cost and location. Find out how top employers view the school. Inquire about the school's placement rate of assisting graduates with job offers. Consider whether you can attend full-time or part-time.

PITFALLS TO PONDER

School is no picnic

When Texas A&M student Tracy Yuan left her steady job as an auditor to pursue an MBA full-time, she thought she'd be "taking some time off from the busy world. I was dreaming of an easy countryside life." Little did she know that it'd be anything but a carefree ride. "The dream was a meltdown with the overwhelming homework, presentation requirements, and exams." Her greatest lesson—both inside and outside the classroom: Graduate school is a lot of hard work. There are no free lunches when it comes to success.

INVESTIGATE OVERSEAS ASSIGNMENTS

Many people share the dream of traveling and working overseas during their lives, but so few know how to make this a reality. There are ways to set yourself apart for these highly competitive positions.

- **Get your passport.** You won't be going anywhere if you don't have it. This small but crucial step can put you in the right frame of mind and dedication it will take to succeed.

- **Travel on your own.** Save your pennies and plan a trip backpacking through Europe. It isn't as pricey as you might think. Not only will you be able to decide if you truly want to devote your career to traveling, but you will gain experience an employer will value.

- **Learn a second language.** Take classes and practice conversations with a native speaker. Find a native speaker, and arrange a "skills trade" where you teach each other your first languages.

- **Join an exchange program.** If you are in school, consider doing an overseas study exchange program. You will learn a lot about different cultures and will make some great networking contacts. Even after you've graduated, many schools offer continuing study programs with the option to study abroad.

- **Know your world politics.** Keep up on world affairs and current events, especially in the country in which you want to travel.

- **Consider teaching English as a second language.** There are many programs and placement agencies to give you information and get you started.

- **Volunteer in a Third World country.** The Peace Corps can give you great career experience and will take you to a wide variety of locations around the world.

- **Sign up for service.** Joining the United States military branches will not only give you traveling experience, but valuable career skills as well. You may also qualify for substantial tuition reimbursement and scholarships.

Jodi Goldman, an HR professional who held overseas assignments in Japan for six years, says an international assignment can be a great way to reinvent yourself. "It can provide you with challenges to help you grow, develop new skills, and shape you into the person you want to become." Goldman has two areas of caution:

First, if your idea of traveling is five-star hotels and restaurants, an overseas assignment might not be as glamorous as you think. Though many companies do send employees to cities such as London and Paris, look to see where your company's offices are. Are these places where you are willing to live, knowing there may be no cable and possible limited access to products from home? You might not have your creature comforts.

If you have a partner or family, make sure they're interested in going as well. Your partner may be at home, unable to work due to visa limitations or raising children, and the support they had in your home country might not be the same overseas. Employees with the most successful overseas assignments are those with partners who are the most adaptive to change.

At this point we hope you have a more thorough picture of how to position your strengths to meet the needs of an employer when applying for a specific position or seeking advancement in your current role. Building on this, chapter 5 will take you one step further by honing your professional etiquette for any environment.

ANSWERS TO QUIZ ON PAGE 63:

1. See today's newspaper for answers.

2. The three branches of the United States government are the Judiciary, Executive, and Legislative.

3. There are 100 members of the United States Senate, two from each state.

4. A bull market is when prices of a certain group of securities are rising or are expected to rise, usually a 15 to 20 percent rise in multiple indexes such as the Dow Jones or the S&P 500. A bear market occurs when prices of a certain group of securities are falling or expected to fall, usually a 15 to 20 percent decline in multiple indexes.

5. The Los Angeles riots were triggered when a predominantly white jury acquitted the four policemen tried in the Rodney King beating case.

6. President Bill Clinton gave "midnight pardons" to 140 people, including his brother, Roger, convicted on cocaine-related charges, his Whitewater partner, Susan McDougal, and financier fugitive Marc Rich whose ex-wife made donations to the Clinton campaign.

7. Libel is false statements of facts about a person that are printed, broadcast, or spoken.

8. Harriet Beecher Stowe wrote *Uncle Tom's Cabin* in 1852.

9. Iraq is on the continent Asia.

10. Napster was a computer file-sharing server accused of violating copyright laws and ordered by the courts to close down.

CHAPTER FIVE

Focus on the Fundamentals
Ace the Essentials of Professional Etiquette

"Beauty fades, dumb lasts forever."

—JUDGE JUDY SHEINDLIN

While it's wise to focus on the big picture, savvy career women never lose sight of the little things that enable us to achieve success on a daily basis. From email and phone skills to dressing for success, we all need to polish our professionalism and ditch the sloppiness. The trend for formality and manners is back. Etiquette is about being comfortable in social and professional situations and making those around you comfortable as well.

Looking the Part

Remember the scene in *Pretty Woman* when none of the sales clerks in the Rodeo Drive boutiques would help Julia Roberts's character? With her tight, ultra-revealing clothes, no one took her seriously, despite having plenty of cash in hand. But when she went back to the same store a few days later, dressed to perfection, sales clerks were falling over themselves to help her. Both times their responses were based purely on attire. Similarly, Tess McGill, the Staten Island assistant played by Melanie Griffith in *Working Girl,* dons her wealthy boss's expensive cocktail attire to grab the attention of a corporate titan. It works: Harrison Ford's character, Jack Trainer, falls for her.

You get the idea: For better or worse, how you dress often determines how people react to you. What you wear can send a message about who you are. Similarly, wearing something inappropriate on an interview or in the workplace can send the wrong signal.

When you're job-hunting, be prepared to meet a networking contact around any corner. You wouldn't want to miss an opportunity to introduce yourself to someone because you were dressed inappropriately. You don't have to walk around every single day in a suit, but take on a business-casual look as the norm when you're looking for a job—even when you're not interviewing.

- Err on the side of conservatism but show some personality, especially at social events.

- Wear clothes that fit and flatter your body type. Don't be too trendy or wear a dress that's intended for your daughter.

- Wear business clothes, not disco attire, to a networking event. Once you have a job, continue your stylish dressing habits.

- Follow the dress code of your office.

- Even with a casual dress code, avoid short skirts, low-cut necklines, too-high heels, too-tight clothes, and anything bordering on the too sexy.

- Store an emergency white blouse in your office in case you spill coffee or even lunch down the front of yourself. These accidents typically happen when you have an important meeting later in the day! Keep an extra pair of hose around, too.

- If you plan to socialize after work and want to bring clothes to change into, be discreet. If co-workers see you in something sexy every Friday after work, you will develop the reputation of a partyer. Fair or not, this reputation carries negative connotations.

- You can dress up your work clothes to go from daytime to evening. Remove your suit jacket to reveal a pretty camisole. Add jewelry and swap flats for heels.

- Buy the right clothes to begin with. If you can't afford a big dry cleaning bill every week, be aware of this when shopping. Buy comfortable shoes you can wear with many outfits.

- Spend a little more money for good quality clothes that will last. These are the clothes you are going to be wearing the majority of the time. They will affect your self-esteem, so it is important that you like them. Pay a few extra dollars to look good and feel great.

- Don't forget hair and makeup. Keep your hair neat, cut, and styled. For rainy days and other mishaps, keep bobby pins and hair holders in your desk. In a pinch, you can also use the hand dryers in the rest room to dry your hair.

- Wear daytime makeup: no heavy eyeliner or glitzy shadows. Lipstick is more flexible, but it is usually better to wear natural shades. Wear makeup that makes you feel beautiful, but only apply it in the privacy of your office or the rest room.

- Jewelry and accessories are your chance to express yourself. Wear jewelry that can serve as a conversation starter. When people pay you a compliment, you can tell them the story of how you got it or where it came from.

Email Maven

You cannot escape email. This tool has revolutionized professional communication, but the simplicity and ease of email can often be misconstrued as an opportunity to be informal and sloppy. There are rules of common courtesy when interacting with people, and electronically is no exception. In fact, rules are doubly important because online you lose visual clues, body language, and tone of voice. Instead of realizing this and making up for the differences, many people write emails that are casual, vague, and unclear in emotion and tone.

PROTECT YOURSELF

- Know your organization's regulations about ownership of email and files. More than likely, your employer retains ownership.

- Assume your messages are not secure and could be read by management at any time. If you wouldn't write it in a postcard, don't write it in an email message. This holds true for your work account as well as any private accounts.

- When forwarding messages, ask for permission first, and don't change the wording. Don't take anything out of context and credit the source. Do not ever forward chain letters or junk mail from your work account.

MANNERS

- Email shouldn't replace personal contact. You might have a conversation and then follow up with an email to confirm what you've discussed.

- If you are upset about something, say it in person or over the phone, not in a heated email.

- Don't write your messages in all caps. THIS INDICATES SHOUTING.

- Check the subjects of all new emails before responding. A person may send you updated information in a subsequent email or may ask you to disregard a previous message.

- Make sure the message was sent to you, and you were not simply cc:ed. If an email conversation has become two-way, don't continue to cc someone else.

- If a message ended up in your mailbox in error, inform the sender of his mistake.

- Be familiar with whom you are sending your emails. Some addresses may appear to be to only one person, but may actually be a list of recipients.

- Your recipients may have different cultures and values, so be sensitive to language, humor, and content.

CONTENT

- Include your contact information in an email, but keep it short: no more than four lines, which include your name, title, email address, and phone number.

- Write a clear subject heading that indicates the content of the message. Use "action required" to request a response or "FYI" if you're just sharing information. The recipients will know how you'd like them to respond.

- Be careful with sarcasm in emails. It usually doesn't work and the recipient may take it literally.

- Formatting is often lost in email, so try to avoid indents, bullets, measurements, and idioms. Use symbols for emphasis (*was* what I meant) and underscores for underlining (_Gone With the Wind_ is my favorite book). Do not use smiley faces in business emails.

- Don't write messages in extra-large fonts or wild colors. This makes it difficult for people to cut and paste your message.

- Double-check all addresses when sending emails.

- Your messages should be brief but understandable and thorough. Double-check spelling and don't use abbreviations or slang.

- When replying to a message, keep the important parts of the original message in your email, but edit out anything irrelevant if length is an issue.

- Be aware of how large a message you are sending. Messages that are too large may not go through.

Keep all emails organized and easy to access in your messaging system, such as Outlook or Hotmail, by creating folders in which to move and save messages. Print hard copies of important emails to ensure safekeeping. Respond to written communication in a timely manner, whether your answer is yes or no, whether you are interested or not. It is rude to leave someone wondering.

Avoid Instant Messaging at work unless it is directly related to work matters. You wouldn't make personal phone calls every few minutes or visit a co-worker's cubicle for small talk every few minutes, so don't Instant Message every few minutes.

The 411 on Phone Calls

Some people love to make personal contact. They know their eye contact, handshake, smile, and body language can be dealmakers. Others prefer the relative anonymity of the telephone. Their strong tools are their sincere voice, professional manner, and to-the-point brevity. There are many of us, however, who would just as soon put a snake to our ear as pick up a telephone, especially to call someone we don't really know. For those phone-a-phobics, here are some tips for easing the stress.

MAKING A CALL

- Think about what you are going to say beforehand. For very important conversations, make a list of the points you want to make, and practice what you want to say. Don't write a script and read it verbatim. Figure out what will grab your audience's attention. Does she volunteer? Build your opening around that. Is he a sports nut? Mention the local team. Sound like you know her when she answers. Talk about him first. Then work yourself into the conversation.

- Before you jump into conversation, ask if it is a good time to talk, or if you can schedule a later time.

- State your points clearly and do not drag on and on. The average person will only be listening to you for about sixty seconds before his mind starts to wander. Say your most important issues first, briefly, and clearly.

- Don't interrupt.

- Listen actively and repeat what she's said back to her so you are certain you understood.

- Determine the next steps or closure before ending the call.

PHONE MANNERS

- Don't bombard people with personal conversations.

- Never raise your voice or use an angry tone even when you are upset. You may regret it later.

- Don't keep anyone on hold for more than a few seconds.

- Don't eat or drink when you are on the phone. This is rude; so is typing during a conversation.

- Don't put someone on speakerphone unless she agrees to it, and make sure to introduce anyone who is listening.

PHONE MESSAGES

Jerry Hocutt, host of Cold Calling for Cowards seminars, says when cold-calling a company, how someone answers the phone will give you clues as to what kind of personality they have. You need to pick up on these cues quickly and respond accordingly. If they are quick, to the point, and no-nonsense, you should be, too. Use this tactic when leaving voicemail messages as well. Listen to their greeting and mimic their tone. You can always listen to their voicemail first, hang up and plan what you want to say, then call back and leave your message.

- When you are leaving a message on voicemail, state your name, company, and phone number at both the beginning and the end of the message, so they do not have to replay the entire message to hear it again.

- Leaving your name and number in a message is not enough. Even if you know the person well, briefly state the purpose of your call.

- Do not leave a message every time you call. Only leave a message if you have new information to provide someone.

- Make your incoming voicemail greeting current and informative. If you'll be out for the day, it's kind to let callers know. "Hi. This is Debbie Beakes. I'm out of the office this week without access to my voicemail. If you need assistance prior to my return, please call Nata Divire at (state your number). Feel free to leave a message and I'll get back to you upon my return. Thank you."

Working 9 to 5

GENERAL BUSINESS ETIQUETTE

Business etiquette is based on hierarchy and power, not gender. The client is always the most important person in business etiquette.

- **Make introductions correctly.** The name of the most important person is said first, regardless of gender.

- **Know when to hold doors.** The person of lesser rank should hold the door for the person of higher rank, regardless of age or gender. In a revolving door, the person of lower rank goes first to get the door moving, and then waits on the other side.

- **The person nearest the elevator door exits first.** In a business setting, the rules of chivalry do not apply, so don't wait for women to exit first, or push past male co-workers.

- **Do not hold chairs for men or women at business functions.** If you think someone physically needs help with their chair, ask before you do anything to avoid embarrassing yourself and them.

- **Only hold coats for clients and those of senior rank.** Don't assume someone will help you into your coat under any circumstances, even if you are of higher rank or are a client. If someone does offer, gracefully accept to avoid an awkward scene.

- **Either party may end a phone conversation.** It's not necessary to wait for the person who called to end a conversation. Once the purpose of the call has been completed, make the move to wrap things up. If the line is disconnected during a call, it is up to the person who placed the call to call back again.

- **Don't offer a handshake across a desk.** When someone visits your office for a meeting, stand up, walk around your desk, and offer a handshake, then indicate exactly where the person should sit. It is better etiquette to offer a seat close to you rather than directly across from you.

GREETING GUESTS

From time to time, you will have guests visit the office, for both personal and work-related reasons. It's important to be ready for them.

- **Tell them where to park.** Make sure guests have directions to your office and know how to locate you once they arrive.

- **Greet them yourself.** Don't leave the greeting responsibilities to the receptionist, especially for special guests. He is more than likely tied to the phones or otherwise busy and can't be as gracious a host as you would like.

- **Be prepared on time and have a place for them to sit right away.** Offer tea, coffee, or water and ask if they need the rest room or anything else, as they may be too shy to bring it up.

- **Keep them entertained.** If they are personal guests, inform them of office rules and procedures. Keep them occupied with magazines or books for adults and coloring or crafts for children.

- **You are responsible for your guests.** Don't let them interrupt anyone's work. Secure permission for them to be there, with indications as to how long and how often. Be familiar with your company's policies on escorting visitors.

When You Are the Guest
- Secure directions, appropriate parking, and arrive on time.

- Announce yourself to the receptionist.

- Bring all supplies and materials.

- Call in advance if you need any special equipment, especially for a meeting or presentation.

- Be prepared with questions and information you want to discuss.

- Do not stretch the meeting over the allotted time.

KEEP IT PERSONAL

It can easily come back to haunt you if you reveal private information about yourself in the workplace—it will shape your co-workers' and your employer's perceptions of you and influence the path of your career. A few years down the road when you want a promotion or salary increase, your employer may not think you are mature or stable enough to handle the position if you continuously discuss your partying, trials, and tribulations. It is simply unprofessional and may embarrass others when you discuss your social life in front of them.

You do not have to hide all the details of your personal life. Just be aware of what you are saying and what it suggests about your personality and capabilities. If you couldn't handle calling a tow truck when your car broke down, your co-workers might think you don't handle stressful situations well and would make a poor manager. If you continuously lose your purse or lock yourself out of your apartment, you might come across as an irresponsible airhead.

The Office Romance

Even though some interoffice romances lead to marriage proposals and wedded bliss, it's not always the case. Meeting people at work is a great way to find someone you have something in common with, and an easy way to get to know someone. But that's where the advantages end and the problems can begin.

If you date a co-worker and then break up, you still have to see this person and get along on a daily basis. There are also the obvious difficulties of dating a subordinate or supervisor. Co-workers will grow resentful and suspicious of any praise, promotions, or favors you give or receive. Often, it is against office policy to date co-workers, and you could both be risking your jobs. It will drag your personal life into the direct spotlight of your co-workers. The co-worker you are dating may innocently, or maliciously, reveal something to the entire office that you would rather keep private.

In researching this book, we heard from many women who had office romances—either with a colleague or a supervisor—and none of them had happy endings. That doesn't mean some relationships don't lead to wedding bells, but these tales can serve as a warning when considering throwing caution—and sometimes a career—to the wind.

Jennifer in New Jersey writes, "I found myself inadvertently flirting with my boss to get his attention on a new project. He responded to my suggestive comments and within days we began a hot and heavy affair. I felt guilty because I know his wife and had even baby-sat for their children. In fact, she's the one who recommended me for this job. Now seven months later I can't break it off without fear of angering him and possibly losing my job. I blame myself for this inappropriate behavior, and I know I've backed myself into this uncomfortable corner. I'm risking my own career and I'm missing out on valuable time that could be spent fostering a healthy relationship with an unmarried man."

Dorothy in Michigan says, "Even though he's single, I made the mistake of getting romantically involved with my boss. We work in a small department and in no time many of our colleagues caught on to our supposedly secretive fling. Adding to the drama, in staff meetings he'd praise my ideas more than others and hand me the most plum assignments. My colleagues were finally fed up with the favoritism and ratted us out to HR. Both of us were reprimanded and reassigned to other departments. Even though we ended the relationship, my reputation was tarnished and it grew increasingly difficult to gain respect and buy-in from teammates. Eventually the stress got to me and I had no choice but to quit. Now I'm job searching and I don't have a great explanation as to why I left that lucrative position."

LUNCH BREAKS

Lunch breaks are an important part of networking. Your behavior at lunch can promote teamwork or can distance you from co-workers. Breaks give you a great opportunity to get to know co-workers from other departments, managers, and other colleagues you wouldn't normally be able to interact with.

- **Follow your co-workers' lead.** If the entire office brings their lunch, bring yours, too, and sit with them. If they go out for lunch, don't wait for them to start inviting you. Invite them. You don't need to know co-workers well to invite them to lunch, so don't be shy.

- **Make a point to invite newcomers to join you.** Not everyone is comfortable inviting him or herself, so make everyone feel welcome.

- **Stick with your budget.** If your co-workers go out to lunch every day and you don't have the money to do so, join them only occasionally. Or recommend restaurants you can afford. If they are not willing to stay in, you may have to go it alone. However, there will surely be someone else who would rather bring her lunch. Eventually someone will follow your lead.

- **Have topics in mind to discuss.** You can discuss any great new restaurants or businesses you have discovered in the area. Popular books, movies, and pop culture icons are also interesting topics.

- **Avoid discussing work.** You can easily annoy co-workers who want to use their break as a break, not a meeting. It can also easily lead to office gossip.

- **Leave every room better than you found it.** Clean up after yourself and take home your utensils and dishes.

DINNER ETIQUETTE

At some point in your career, you will encounter the business lunch or dinner, whether with clients or co-workers. Though it may seem like a casual setting, don't let your guard down. You are still at work.

- Go to the rest room ahead of time. You don't want to excuse yourself right in the middle of the meal unless it is necessary.

- Sit with your feet flat on the floor or crossed at your ankles only.

- Wait for your supervisor to unfold her napkin before you do, as she is the host. Gently place it in your lap.

- Order appropriately—not too expensive, but not the cheapest thing on the menu either. Now is not the time to be a picky eater.

- Don't drink alcohol, even if your manager orders it for herself. If someone orders alcohol for you, don't refuse, but be careful of drinking it.

- Wait for everyone to be served before eating.

- Use silverware in the order it is placed on the table, from the outside to the inside. Use the butter knife if provided.

- Once you have picked up a utensil, do not set it back on the table. Rest it on your plate.

- It's proper etiquette to use your bread to push peas and other small foods onto your fork. Just don't use your thumb.

- Don't chew and talk at the same time. If you are asked a question while you have food in your mouth, swallow and then answer. It's okay to pause for a few seconds.

- Try not to ask a question right when someone takes a bite of food.

- Condiments are passed to the right, food to the left. Always pass the salt and pepper together, even if only one was requested.

- If you absolutely must get up, place your napkin on your seat, not on the table.

- Do not make a phone call and leave your cell phone turned off. If you are expecting an important call, forward it on to someone else.

- Just in case, bring along enough money to cover both your meal and other guests'. It would be embarrassing to not have the money to pay if the situation arose.

BREAKING BAD HABITS

Common tics involve the hands, mouth, or lips, such as twirling hair, chewing pens and pencils, cracking knuckles, jingling keys and change, or biting nails or lips. Tics tend to come across as unprofessional, demonstrate a lack of confidence, and can be distracting to others. To break a habit, consider these steps:

- Identify the circumstances under which you perform the tic, such as times, situations, and emotional states. If you can anticipate when you will perform the tic, then you're more apt to prevent it.

- Choose a behavior you can perform instead of the tic or to interrupt it, such as placing your palms together, blowing through your lips, or placing your feet flat on the floor. Ask someone to point out when you're performing your tic so you can replace it with your substitute behavior.

- Set up a reward system that motivates you to quit the habit. It must be a reward you really want, such as a new dress. Don't accept the reward until you've broken the habit.

OFFICE PARTIES AND GIFT-GIVING

Office parties are still about business, no matter how small the office and no matter how close of friends you are with your co-workers. At company functions, you must behave professionally. You can dramatically hurt your reputation and professionalism even in one night.

- **Dress appropriately.** Anything revealing should stay at home. Dress to maintain the image you want co-workers and employers to have of you.

- **Drink alcohol in moderation or not at all.** You may end up embarrassing yourself.

- **Introduce yourself.** Office parties may be one of the rare occasions when you see your company's CEO or president. Don't just mingle with your regular office buddies.

- **Be a gracious guest of honor.** If you are honored with a toast, do not drink to yourself or clap when others applaud you. Make a toast to the person who toasted you to thank them for the recognition.

- **Thank the person who organized the party.** They put in a lot of hard work to make the event a success for your enjoyment.

In Charge of Planning the Party?

- Respect everyone's cultures and beliefs. A "holiday party" is more appropriate than a "Christmas party."

- Be aware of the time of day you schedule the party for. You want to ensure that the majority can attend. If you have it during office hours, make sure no one is stuck working. If the majority of staffers have children who must be picked up from childcare, then six P.M. isn't the ideal time either.

- Review your company's policy on serving alcohol at company-sponsored events.

- Make it very clear on the invitation who is invited, and whether or not children, spouses, and other guests are welcome.

Gracious Gift-Giving

Office gift-giving can easily get out of control. Unless you want to end every holiday season completely broke, take charge of the situation now.

As a general rule, it is sometimes inappropriate to give your boss a gift. However, some rules are meant to be broken, so you should follow the protocol established in your office. If you are a close personal friend, save the gift exchange for after work hours. Usually, the entire office will go in together to give the boss a present. If the idea of a group gift does not come up, you can be the one to initiate it.

IT WORKS FOR ME

Take charge ·

"The entire office was invited to our boss's wedding. The office decided to pool our money to get her a new desk chair. I was appalled by the choice of the present as I felt that a desk chair was not a considerate gift for a wedding, especially because it excluded the groom completely. So, I decided to 'take charge' of the wedding gift. I circulated an email asking people if they would rather get her the chair or a gift certificate to a major department store. Everyone voted and decided on the gift certificate, which suited the couple more appropriately." —Sydney Keith, designer in Salt Lake City, Utah

If you are asked to donate money to a pool for an expectant mother, retiree, or anyone else, donate the requested money unless it poses a serious financial burden on you. More than likely it will be no more than $20, so consider it a good investment for peace of mind and your reputation. If you really can't afford to contribute, say so and donate what you *can* afford, even if it is only a few dollars.

A few other guidelines for office gift-giving:

- If you have an assistant, buy her a holiday gift. A company bonus does not count as a gift.

- Unless you are giving a gift to everyone, give your gifts privately.

- Consider giving your best clients and customers a corporate gift, such as a basket of teas or high-quality chocolates.

- Don't feel obligated to give everyone a gift. Only give a gift in the true spirit of giving, which is to express your thanks or to honor someone.

- The best gifts in the workplace do not take a lot of creativity. Everyone likes gift certificates and food products. Opt for safe bets, but consider the recipients' interests.

- When you receive a gift, make sure you send a thank-you note.

ETIQUETTE QUIZ

Put your own manners to the test to see how you stack up in professional etiquette. Take this quiz to review what you've learned in this chapter.

_____ 1. Your colleague gave you tickets to an industry-related seminar she was unable to attend. You showed up half an hour late and the door was barred, so you missed the speakers. Should you:

    A. Apologize in person and send a thank-you.

    B. Send her a thank-you for the tickets and not mention that you missed the seminar.

    C. Send her a thank-you for the tickets that explains what happened.

    D. Send her an apology note.

_____ 2. You are invited to attend a work banquet and are excited for the chance to network with people from every department. The problem is you are vegetarian and the menu for the event is prime rib. Should you:

    A. Show up late so you miss the dinner but are able to network afterwards.

    B. Eat beforehand, and then nibble on the salad and vegetable dishes.

    C. Explain to your server you do not eat meat and ask for a vegetarian plate.

    D. Explain to the people around you why you are not eating.

_____ 3. Every year your office has a sign-up sheet for employees who want to be involved in a "Secret Santa" gift exchange. You signed up and gave a nice gift to a co-worker, but mysteriously did not receive one from your "Secret Santa." Should you:

    A. Confront the person you are certain was supposed to be your "Secret Santa," because you are sure they don't like you and did it to be malicious.

B. Tell your supervisor.

C. Just forget about it and not sign up the next year.

D. Assume it was a mistake and forward along an email asking if anyone received two gifts.

_____ 4. **Your co-workers Instant Message you all the time and it is interrupting your work schedule. What should you do?**

A. Simply ignore them until you have time to deal with them.

B. Politely request that people only I.M. you when it is very important.

C. Read them and quickly send a message as to when you will respond in detail.

D. Block them. They can send you an email the "old-fashioned" way.

_____ 5. **You arrive at the office where you are to be interviewed. The receptionist greets you and shows you to the room where you are to have the interview. It has been twenty minutes since you have seen anyone. What should you do?**

A. Ask the receptionist how much longer it will be and whether you can reschedule the interview.

B. Wait ten more minutes before you decide to do anything.

C. Leave and call later that afternoon.

D. Not worry about it and use the time to review your résumé and answers to difficult questions.

_____ 6. **You went to a job interview that you thought went well. You called when you said you would but did not get a hold of your interviewer. You called the next day, and the day after that. You left messages but still have not gotten a response. What should you do?**

A. Call again the next day.

B. Ask the receptionist if the position has been filled.

C. Ask when you would be able to get a hold of the person. Ask for the person's email address and send an email.

D. Accept defeat.

ANSWERS

1. A. It is best to own up to your mistake and explain you missed the speakers. She may ask you how it was, or may find out from someone else who attended the event that you weren't there. Never apologize in a note. It will seem insincere and cowardly.

2. B. Making an issue out of your vegetarian views, either by mentioning them or requesting a vegetarian plate, may make others around you uncomfortable. Graciously accept what is offered to you and only eat what you'd like.

3. D. Try to get to the bottom of the gift-giving issue without accusing anyone. More than likely it was just a mistake. But don't just let it go. You put in a lot of money and effort to participate with the understanding that it would be returned to you.

4. B. You can't risk ignoring or blocking unwanted Instant Messages, and sending a quick note as to when you will reply is still a distraction. The only way to truly solve the problem is to politely ask that your co-workers refrain from contacting you this way, since it's a distraction. Still, the best bet is to turn off your I.M. until after hours.

5. A. Don't sit around for half an hour without mentioning anything. There may have been a misunderstanding. If you've run out of time, certainly reschedule, but don't leave without figuring out where your interviewer is.

6. C. Don't give up simply because your phone calls aren't returned. They may be having a very busy week. Instead, switch tactics so you aren't hounding them with calls. Maybe they are easier to get a hold of by email.

*   *   *

Even though a whole bunch of rules can feel overwhelming, following professional etiquette ensures that you won't offend anyone, and that you will actually impress the people you interact with. Being successful *and* polite is a winning combination.

CHAPTER SIX

Win (Don't Whine) Your Way Ahead
Cooperating with Colleagues
and Clients Is Key

"The way I see it, if you want the rainbow, you gotta put up with the rain."
—DOLLY PARTON

Way back in kindergarten we were taught to respect others, wait our turn, share, be patient, and be on our best behavior unless we wanted to spend the afternoon in the time-out chair watching everyone else have fun. Well, unfortunately, some people never caught on. In this chapter, we will advise you how to deal with these people and what to do if you're—gulp—one of them.

Mastering interpersonal skills and behaviors is key to career success. The higher up the career ladder you climb, the more important it becomes to not only master skills and technical know-how, but social and "people" skills as well. Outstanding interpersonal skills can make a good candidate a great one.

The Basics of Good Behavior

RESPECT ALL CULTURES

Unless you live in the middle of nowhere, you will more than likely encounter people with different beliefs and cultures from yours in the workplace. *Everyone* has to learn to accept others' differences.

- Don't try to push your values or beliefs on anyone. Respect that it may be against coworkers' cultures to celebrate birthdays, holidays, or other office "extras."

- Try to find a way to include everyone. Instead of birthdays, have a "monthly celebration" with cake and ice cream to cover all special events.

- If you are curious about someone's culture or are afraid you're offending them, simply ask. They might be happy for the chance to explain.

- Don't get angry or defensive about your culture and beliefs. If you were slighted, chances are it wasn't intentional. Give people the benefit of the doubt and sit down with them for a serious conversation if something's upsetting you.

PROVIDE CUSTOMER SERVICE

"Quality is remembered long after the price is forgotten."
—GUCCI FAMILY SLOGAN

In most areas of our careers, we are taught to put our needs first, be assertive, and ask for what *we* want. Well, by providing great customer service—by putting someone's needs above your own, at least outwardly—we often get what we want in return.

- **Apologize and don't argue.** If a client—internal or external—comes to you with a complaint, acknowledge it, apologize, admit you were wrong, and fix the problem. Debating or haggling over the issue will only escalate the problem, making your customer even more upset. Let them vent.

- **Ask for feedback.** Provide clients an opportunity to rate your service on a regular basis through a questionnaire or other form of evaluation. Inform them that you value their feedback and offer the evaluation as a chance to improve your service in the future.

- **Accommodate special requests.** If a client asks to move up a deadline, changes their mind on some of the details, or wants to meet after hours or on a weekend, do your best to accommodate their needs. This may mean giving up social plans once in a while, traveling on the spur of the moment, or even requesting the service of another professional. For example, if you work for a caterer, a customer may call the day before the event and ask to increase the amount of food by a significant amount. You need to accommodate these requests if you want them as a customer in the future.

- **Keep your promises and go the extra mile.** If you promise a customer something will be completed by a certain date, make sure it is. Create a cushion in what you estimate the price and deadline to be, so you have room to maneuver if necessary. A customer will be much more impressed if you bring a project in under deadline and under cost than if it is late. Don't ever promise what you know you can't deliver.

 IT WORKS FOR ME

Above and beyond at all hours

"When professionals will work with the client's time zone to make sure that matters are handled expediently, it's often a differentiating factor that translates to success on the job. I have frequently gotten up to make calls to foreign lands at 2:30 A.M. to assure the client that I was able to be available at the beginning of their workday and not an obstacle to the timeliness of the business deal." —Ann Newton, partner at Houston-based law firm Hayes and Boone

THE POWER OF PERSUASION

The power of persuasion is not to be underestimated. It comes to some naturally. Once you have mastered it, you are well on your way to being heard.

- **Raise your expectations.** You are more likely to get something if you expect it. A doubting attitude will result in a halfhearted effort. For example, rather than merely *hoping* that a co-worker will complete his portion of your team's project, speak directly to him to confirm your expectations on the contents and deadline.

- **Persistence is key.** Don't give up if co-workers first reject your ideas. Simply revise your plan, address their concerns, and try again.

- **Compromise.** Decide what has the highest value for you and what you can negotiate. People are more likely to do things your way, if they can have something their way, too.

IT ISN'T PERSONAL

From time to time, you will feel rejected or snubbed at work. Anyone who takes pride in her work will have a hard time dealing with criticism every now and then. The way you handle failure and criticism says a lot about your integrity and professionalism.

- **Allow your ego time to heal.** Usually, the first response to criticism is denying its validity. At first, it may sting too much to evaluate criticism fairly.

- **Think about what was said.** Evaluate the criticism and see your work from someone else's point of view. What was the critic's point?

- **Give the criticism the benefit of the doubt.** Accept for a moment that it is true. What can you do to correct the situation?

- **Make some changes.** Implement these corrections and learn from the criticism.

- **Do not dismiss criticisms as nitpicky.** You may have completed your work very well, but you can always add polish. Perfect the details, too.

- **Don't take it personally.** Realize they are not criticizing you, but your work. Since everyone sees things differently, it's important to adapt.

- **Keep it in perspective.** Just because you failed on one book assignment does not mean that you are a failure as an editor. You may not like every one of Ralph Lauren's shirts, but overall he's still a renowned designer.

- **Believe in yourself.** Have enough self-worth that you can accept it when others do not view you or your work in a positive light.

- **Consider the source.** Is the person critiquing you an expert? Was the criticism meant to be constructive, or just mean? Many people, including managers, have not learned to give feedback tactfully, so take the message and leave the insults.

- **Be aware of your professional level.** If you are criticized for not knowing something a senior-level professional should know, but you are only a mid-level professional, don't take it to heart. Consider it a positive sign that you are on the cusp of higher achievement.

COMMUNICATE

An office won't run smoothly without good communication, so do your part. Most problems could be eliminated, or even prevented, with a little communication. To be successful in business, it's essential to make yourself heard. Don't assume it's someone else's responsibility to listen to what you've got to say; the burden is on you to be an effective communicator.

IT WORKS FOR ME

Kids say the darndest things

Kindergarten teacher Suzanne Blank teaches this little ditty about proper manners to her students at Manhattan School for Children. While it's more exciting to hear it sung by innocent five-year-olds than to read it in black and white, the lesson of this short verse applies to the boardroom as much as it does to the playground.

> *If you ever have a problem, a problem, a problem,*
> *If you ever have a problem, let's talk it out.*
> *Let's look at the choices, and speak in calm voices,*
> *If you ever have a problem, let's talk it out.*

- **Communicate with team members and supervisors.** Let them know what you're working on so no one duplicates your efforts and supervisors can help you prioritize. Let everyone know when you have completed a project. Others may be waiting for you to finish your step so they can begin theirs.

- **Know who needs to know.** Have a general knowledge about everyone's position within the company. When something comes up that is not your domain, take the information to the right person.

- **Speak up.** Whether you have a complaint or a great idea, voice your opinion in a professional tone. Your ideas can benefit the company as a whole, not to mention gain you the reputation of a valuable asset and source of information.

- **Watch your language.** There is no room for slang or curse words in the workplace, even at social gatherings with co-workers.

We're on the same team

"Several years ago the technology company that I was working for acquired another tech firm. I came into work one day to find a lady sitting in my area who said that she had the same title as I did, and she had been told to fly to our offices and begin work. You can imagine the look on my face.

"At first we were really at odds with each other, but after a few days, we decided to approach management together. We found out that through the acquisition, no one had thought about duplication within the marketing department! After our meeting, she and I sat down and decided who was a best fit for which projects and we just moved on." —Caroline Brown, marketing manager for a Fortune 100 company

LEARNING TO LISTEN

An old proverb says "God gave us two ears but only one mouth because listening is twice as hard as talking." People like to hear about themselves, so involve them in your story, too. Don't say, "I had a wonderful time at the event last night." Instead ask, "Didn't you have the most marvelous time at the event?" Listen to others and they will listen to you. Nothing gratifies a person more than being accepted and listened to. A few don'ts for success as a listener:

- Don't let your prejudices get in the way. Listen with an open mind.

- Don't be so busy readying your answer that you don't really hear the other person's point.

- Don't think you know what they're going to say before they say it.

- Don't be afraid to ask someone to repeat something you haven't understood.

- Don't show that you aren't paying attention.

Might Your Attitude Need Realignment?

Sometimes your trouble at work might not be the fault of your co-workers. Perhaps some of your challenges may require you to look at your own attitude and behavior and consider making adjustments to accommodate not only other people, but your own success as well.

LEAVE THE DOORMAT AT THE DOOR

There are co-workers who will try to take advantage of you any way they can, especially if you have a reputation as a pushover. For example, if you're known as someone who's quiet and reserved, others may feel entitled to speak up and take credit for your ideas. If you enjoy picking up coffee for yourself midday, others might peg you as the gopher for their needs. It is crucial to stop this behavior from the beginning, so you do not become the target of their bullying.

This can be difficult for most people, because standing up for ourselves often feels like nitpicking. Most of us have learned to let the little things slide and to compromise and cooperate. But if you consistently let things slide with your co-workers, you risk becoming a doormat—and everyone will take advantage of you, not just the bullies.

Quite often, if you simply point out someone's behavior, they will stop. Simply say, "I was concerned that you were twenty minutes late returning from lunch, which pushes my lunch break time back. Is everything ok?" Then politely ask them to respect the schedules. Bringing it up will make them aware that you will no longer ignore their disrespectful actions.

If you are the one who always takes out the trash, ask someone to do it and explain that you did it the day before. Offer a schedule of shared responsibility, so it's clear that you're not looking to get out of doing your part. If someone begs for your front-row tickets to the baseball game, tell them how excited you are to use them, and where they can get their own. The goal is to be polite, but firm.

If you have the reputation of a doormat, it may take people by surprise when you start to stand up for yourself. They may even become angry (unjustifiably) about your new spine. It will get easier with time, not only because you will get better at standing up for yourself, but because your co-workers will no longer perceive you as someone to take advantage of.

OVERCOME YOUR SHYNESS

Another behavior that will get you nowhere in the workplace is shyness. Your co-workers can sometimes misinterpret your shyness as aloofness or an air of superiority. Shyness will separate you from the group and prevent you from succeeding. How will you ever manage your own team if you are too shy to lead them? How will you ever ask for the raise and promotion you deserve if you are too shy to speak to your boss?

Sometimes shyness is simply an innate part of your personality. You may have all the confidence in the world about your appearance, skills, and abilities, but are simply shy on an interpersonal level. To change your character, practice visualization. Visualization is the technique of "cognitively practicing" the behavior you wish to have. Shyness is a mind-set. To change it, you must practice trying on a new mind-set.

In the privacy and comfort of your own home, where you will not be interrupted and can feel completely relaxed, find a place where you can lie still and visualize. Start small. Don't try to visualize yourself as the center of attention right off the bat. Kick off your shoes, change into comfortable clothing, and get into a "quiet mood." Once you are fully relaxed, follow these six steps of visualization.

1. Close your eyes and picture a situation at work when you feel shy. What is happening that makes you feel shy? Are you around someone in particular? Are you asked to speak or perform a responsibility? Do you feel like there are people watching you?

2. If you are remembering a specific scene that happened in the past, try to remember it as accurately as possible. Who was there, and what made you feel shy?

3. What did you say? What did your supervisor and co-workers say? What about your behavior do you feel was inadequate? What did you do wrong or not do well enough?

4. Now, replay the scene in your head, only substitute the behaviors you wish you had performed. Say what you would have liked yourself to say. If you cannot think of how you could have changed the situation, think about someone you admire. What would they have done differently in that situation? Now picture yourself doing that.

5. Imagine how your co-workers would have responded to your "new" behavior. What would they have said or done? Continue picturing the scenario while inserting your "improved behavior" until the interaction is complete.

6. Picture yourself in a setting in the future when you do not want to be shy, such as an upcoming meeting or personal evaluation. Who will be there? Do you know this person? What will they ask you? What will they bring? Where will you be? What will you be wearing? What noises will you hear? Think of answers you would like to give to any difficult questions. Picture yourself acting and responding in a friendly, outgoing manner. Picture yourself feeling comfortable and confident. Play out the scene step by step until you come out successfully.

Twenty to thirty minutes of visualization a day will gradually help you interact more comfortably with your co-workers. Even if you find such detailed visualization difficult at first, do not give up. It will become easier with practice.

BE ASSERTIVE

If you ever want to become a leader, manager, or supervisor, you need to learn to become assertive. You need to assertively ask others to do things, and you need to assertively say yes or no to co-workers' requests.

Don't confuse being assertive with aggressive or passive-aggressive behavior. Assertive means making a positive statement and giving solid reasons. Aggressive means controlling or abusing, making a negative statement, or shouting insults and accusations. Passive means asking questions or avoidance. Passive-aggressive means hitting below the belt, not confronting the issue, but retaliating in a way that can't be seen.

Assertive: I would like to schedule a meeting with you on Monday to go over the project.

Aggressive: I can't believe you haven't shown me the project yet. Meet with me Monday.

Passive: What are you doing on Monday?

Passive-aggressive: Scheduling a meeting for Monday without telling your co-worker.

Turn the following aggressive statements into assertive ones:

- You always leave the break room a mess.

- Give me those documents.

- You look terrible when you wear that to work.

- You better have that done by Friday.

Turn the following passive statements into assertive ones:

- I wonder why nobody cleans up the break room.

- I hope the documents will be ready sometime soon.

- Some people shouldn't wear short skirts to work.

- Let's hope it's all done by the end of the week.

Turn the following passive-aggressive statements into assertive ones:

- Some idiot keeps leaving documents in the copier.

- Somebody's car was blocking me in so I called a tow truck.

- The coat closet was a mess so I threw a bunch of stuff out.

- I'm leaving if the client isn't here in a few minutes.

To be assertive, you must be clear about what you want and expect, and why. You are not asking as much as you are stating. You are not attacking. You are communicating clearly and effectively.

PITFALLS TO PONDER

Know your place

After two great interviews with an employer, a summer intern surprised her colleagues with strange behavior on her very first day. She was eerily quiet for the first two hours, and then stood up and launched loudly into this laundry list of "problems" with the office: Why is CNBC on all day since it's boring and distracting? Why is the air conditioning kept so cool when people work harder when they're sweating? Why are the phones answered on the second or third ring instead of letting it go to voicemail to give callers the illusion that everyone is busy and unavailable? Needless to say, they were taken aback by her attack on a relatively normal office environment.

She ended the tirade in tears and explained that she'd been given advice to "speak out" and "make opinionated observations" as a way to gain notice and kudos on the job. What she wasn't told—or what she chose not to follow—is that there's a time, place, and method for making your thoughts known. Rude outbursts are rarely, if ever, the way to go.

COOL YOUR TEMPER

If you consistently lose your temper, your co-workers and supervisors will see you as someone who is angry and has no self-control. If you lose your temper, your likeability and credibility will follow.

- **Establish a balance between your emotional side and your rational side.** Emotions come easily and naturally. They are a response. The rational side requires thought.

- **Don't let people egg you on.** You may encounter co-workers who actually *try* to make you lose your temper. It is a tactic of manipulation. Once you fall for it, you will quite often say or do things that will hurt your own performance and help theirs in comparison.

The goal is not to no longer feel angry, but to no longer show the outside world just how angry you really are. Anger is communicated through body language, behavior, and voice: all things you can control. To control your temper, you have to be aware of what you say and do and what your body language is communicating to others.

When someone upsets or offends you, your first reaction is often to blurt out some kind of nasty comment. Since it's impossible to take back your words, it's smart to always resist the urge to speak before you think. When someone says or does something that makes you angry, instead of responding, take a deep breath and don't say a word until your anger subsides and your rational side kicks back in. A few things to remember:

- **It really is just business.** Even if it seems personal, it is about work. Do not take it personally and try not to be insulted.

- **Gain control.** Once your emotions have cooled, speak in a controlled tone and use rational responses and logic, rather than defensive arguments and insults. The more you keep your cool, the more likely the person attacking you will lose theirs. You win. You always win by keeping your temper in check.

It is not as easy to control your body language, facial expressions, and actions. It takes more practice because like your emotions, they are reactions. While you are taking a few deep breaths to calm down, consciously run through a checklist from head to toe.

- Is your face relaxed? You need not be smiling, but lose the grimace.

- Keep your shoulders back and have good posture, but do not lean in or assume a threatening stance.

- Where are your hands? Do not make fists, or prop them on your hips in an angry pose.

- Don't tap your feet, drum your fingers, or give any other signs that you are tense and upset.

- Keep still and consciously say to yourself, "I am cool, calm, and collected."

Think of losing your temper as blowing your cover. Every time you lose your temper, a little piece of your fort crumbles away and you are more vulnerable to the stones others may throw. No matter how "justified" you are in losing your temper, it is not professional behavior.

 **IT WORKS FOR ME**

Patience is a virtue

When your patience runs short, try these short solutions:

1. Keep a paperclip in your pocket. When you get angry or lose your patience, move the paperclip from one pocket to the other, to interrupt your anger and focus your thoughts on something else.
2. 3, 2, 1, BLASTOFF! Well, hold the blastoff, but count down from ten before you speak. Use the time to think about how important it is to remain in control.
3. Meditate to the sound of the phone. On the first ring, breathe in deeply. At the second ring, exhale and either pick it up or leave it to voicemail.
4. Try the Raggedy Ann exercise. Scoot your chair away from your desk, sit forward in your seat, and let your arms, head, and neck fall toward the floor freely. Imagine all the tension flowing into the floor.

IT'S NOT ALL COMPETITION

Unhealthy competition is a source of conflict in the workplace. "People have a tendency to compare themselves against what everyone else is doing and what they're receiving as a reward. This is a constant source of frustration to managers," says Tracy Johnson, vice president of human resources for the Allegis Group. "If some people put as much effort into their work as they do worrying about what everyone else is doing, they would be much more productive." Johnson encourages her staffers to concentrate on

BOOK BREAK

Michael Gelman, the successful executive producer of *Live with Regis & Kelly*, who's often seen on-camera kibitzing with the two hosts, enjoyed reading *The Way of the Ronin: Riding the Waves of Change at Work* (Ronin Publishing, 1988) because "it captures great points and offers innovative career strategies" for getting ahead in an unpredictable workplace.

their strengths and request projects and tasks that will highlight them.

Johnson also advises employees to talk to their managers about themselves, and not others. "It's a turnoff when an employee comes to me and says they're upset and don't understand why a co-worker got to work on something." She says a better alternative is for the person to approach her by saying they heard about this exciting project and would love to be considered for similar work in the future. "This gives me the opportunity to talk to the employee about their interests, skills, and future instead of forcing me to defend my decisions."

MEETINGS

Meetings are an important part of communication and teamwork. For a meeting to be a success, everyone must contribute and participate actively. Otherwise, meetings can quickly become a waste of everyone's time. When attending a meeting:

- **Read and review all materials beforehand.** Bring the proper materials with you. Know the agenda and topics of discussion well, and do any research necessary so you are up to speed.

- **Show up on time.** Not only is arriving late rude and disruptive, you can miss important information.

- **Don't bring your cell phone to a meeting.** It just invites disruption; leave it at your desk or in your purse and turned off.

- **Always bring a pen and paper.** Take good notes so you can remember everything and will know how to proceed. Make lists.

- **Listen attentively in meetings and participate.** A meeting is not the time to space out or daydream about last night's movie. It is rude not to listen to those who are speaking, and you can learn or build off of other people's ideas.

- **Don't interrupt others when they are speaking.** It breaks down communication, and is very rude to boot. Even if you are upset by something, hold your tongue until the person has finished speaking.

- **Voice your opinion, whether you are in favor of something or not.** Even if your opinion has already been added to the conversation, you need to let the group know what you are thinking. It is important to get a good picture of what the majority is thinking, so do your part.

- **Ask questions when you are still in the meeting.** Other people may have similar questions.

- **Never walk out confused.** Be clear on the next steps and how to proceed based on the meeting's outcome.

Leading a meeting is a great opportunity to develop leadership skills and demonstrate your knowledge.

- Dress appropriately, just a step nicer than what you would normally wear to a meeting.

- Be prepared with the right documents, visual aids, and a smooth, clear speech. Test-drive equipment before the meeting to ensure it is working properly and you know how to use it. Have a backup plan in case it doesn't.

- When appropriate, circulate an agenda in advance to inform co-workers of the purpose of the meeting. Include a list of items they need to bring, research they need to conduct, or projects that need to be completed beforehand. Make sure you give them the time to prepare what you are asking them to bring as well as any agenda items they might have. Leave time for others to speak and ask questions. A meeting should be an open discussion of ideas, so provide the information and open the floor for debate.

- It is up to you to keep everyone's attention and to steer the course of the meeting. If people look bored or don't seem to be paying attention, take a break, ask for their feedback, or pose a question to get them thinking again. Keep control of the discussion to make the meeting as efficient as possible, and to ensure everything that needs to be addressed is discussed. Don't let people get off track. If an idea has already been discussed and decided upon, don't let the conversation linger on that subject.

- You are in charge of making sure the meeting doesn't run into overtime. Wrap things up in a timely fashion.

RESPECT CO-WORKERS' SPACE

Don't enter or rummage through someone else's workspace, even in cubicles. It may be tempting just to go in and grab something you need, but it could potentially get you in trouble. Ask for permission first and go in only the drawers and areas specified. Your co-workers may have personal items in their desk and you might unknowingly disorganize something important. If something comes up missing, you don't want to be held in question.

Be careful of where you place things on others' desks as well. Put borrowed items back where they belong, messages where they will be seen, documents in the "in-box," and lunch or beverages on the corner of the desk where it won't seep onto something important.

- Keep your voice at an appropriate level, especially in cubicles.

- Avoid making personal calls that co-workers can overhear.

- Don't voice all of your thoughts and ideas simply because someone is within hearing range.

When covering for a co-worker on vacation:

• Keep her files and documents organized in the same manner she normally does, even if it is not the system *you* use.

• Take good notes of what has been done, and save all emails and correspondence so she can easily pick up where you leave off.

• Take her responsibilities as seriously as you take your own.

• When she returns, walk her through everything you covered while she was gone. Be prepared to answer questions on an ongoing basis.

BUILD YOUR REPUTATION

Your reputation, by definition, is something you must build up over time. It is an overall, general assumption others make about your actions and personality. It is the information others will use to judge how you will act in the future. "From the day we are born, we begin setting the groundwork for our lifelong reputation. This holds true for both our personal and business lives," says Mike Paul, president of MGP & Associates PR. "Every one of our actions is layered into a dossier that can be produced years later for someone to make an assessment of our credibility, our track record and ultimately our reputation. Consider, for example, the appointment of Senator Joe Lieberman as Al Gore's Vice President selection on the Democratic ticket in 2000. Everything from Lieberman's third-grade teacher's assessment of him to his condemnation of President Clinton's indiscretions with Monica Lewinsky seemed to form the basis of his selection."

You can't achieve a good reputation overnight. A good reputation isn't just built on words alone; it's built on actions as well. You must work hard, consistently. And it will pay off with a good reputation.

• **Develop a good reputation.** Continuously perform your job responsibilities, but more than that, consistently give a little more. Volunteer to run an errand for the boss. Be the one who knows how to change the toner in the copy machine and the ink in the printer. Work on the weekends. You don't necessarily have to perform enormous tasks all the time, but perform a string of little "extras" that everyone appreciates. Bring donuts every once in a while!

• **Avoid a bad reputation.** In contrast, a bad reputation takes very little time to acquire. It really only takes one day or one stupid action to ruin your reputation. Show up to the office party wearing a short, tight dress, get drunk and flirt with every man in the room, and your reputation for professionalism is ruined. People may forgive, but there are certain things they just won't forget.

• **Damage control.** Reputations stick. If you develop a bad reputation early on, it will be very hard to recover. Even though you should own up to mistakes and apologize for indiscretions, keep in mind that even years of good behavior will not erase that one time you really screwed up. The best you can do is start now to develop a new pattern of behavior. If you really need a fresh start, consider changing positions or companies.

Start working on your reputation now and hold onto it with both hands. Guard it seriously. "Reputations are more vulnerable than ever with the voracious appetite of 24/7 news outlets and the Internet for content," Mike Paul says. "Clearly, our reputations are up for grabs. Today we are all a mouse-click away from someone attempting to tarnish our good name. As the owner of a good reputation, it is imperative that you take a look at your weaknesses and shore up any frailties with swift, aggressive responses."

DEVELOP LEADERSHIP SKILLS

"There are too many women taking orders and not enough giving orders."
—CAROLYN MALONEY, (D-NY) U.S. Representative

When you are the leader all eyes are on you, so act accordingly at all times. People look to you for example, and will judge you more quickly and harshly than other team members. Be a woman of action, not words. Set an example of productivity, organization, and responsibility. To be a great leader, develop the following skills:

- **Mind your Ps and Qs.** It is not what you do, but also the way you do it that makes a good leader. Do not step on toes and don't lead in a detrimental way. Show others you are decisive and don't beat around the bush.

- **Be knowledgeable.** As the leader, you should know more about the job than the rest of the team. Make decisions based on facts and research. Do not boast about your smart moves until after the results have come back successful, or you will risk looking like a fool. If you do make a mistake, acknowledge it and move on.

- **Don't show emotion.** Don't overcelebrate your successes, as you will lose respect. Don't dwell on your losses or become stoic.

- **Develop your speaking skills.** When you address a group, you need to sound clear and confident to infuse others with confidence in your ability. Great speakers have learned to combine poise and polish with charisma and intelligence. Don't ramble on or stutter. Stand tall and look your audience in the eye.

- **Dress successfully.** You should always look top-notch. How you look is a large part of people's perceptions of you.

PITFALLS TO PONDER

Handling heated disagreements and other conflicts

"When two employees have a conflict, managers should always remember that there are many sides to every story. Managers shouldn't take sides, but rather act as an independent mediator," advises Jennifer Sullivan of CareerBuilder.com. "Invite both employees into your office. Have Employee A tell Employee B what he/she thought the other one said or did and vice versa. Because both employees are present, they are less likely to exaggerate details. They are also less likely to react inappropriately with the manager present. The manager can listen objectively and let the employees talk through the issue and find a resolution."

Leading a Project

As the leader of a team or committee, it is your job to direct a cohesive, productive project. The responsibility for failure of the assignment falls directly on your shoulders. So do the potential rewards for your success.

- Focus on the end goal. Do not let the project take on a life of its own and steer in the wrong direction.

- Invite discussions and solutions from all team members

- Assign tasks to each team member. Make sure the work is distributed evenly and fairly and that every detail is accounted for.

- Stay flexible. Be prepared for snags and setbacks. Allow each member to take pride and creativity in their own task.

- Trust the team. Check in for progress and details. Do not micromanage.

- Pull the details together for a final project.

- Ask for feedback from team members.

Embrace new assignments

"My boss once pulled me out of an area in which I excelled and gave me responsibility for several departments I had little to no experience in. My co-worker was given full responsibility for the area I most enjoyed and felt most comfortable with. I was disappointed, but didn't want to show that to my manager. However, I couldn't just let it go without some discussion, so I told him I was a little nervous about taking on the new responsibilities. I asked if he was sure pulling me from the department in which I excelled was the best thing.

"He told me he wanted me to get exposure to these other areas because, strategically, I needed to show I was well-rounded in all the areas of human resources if I ever wanted to be in his position. I appreciated his vote of confidence, and that conversation allowed me to pursue the new job with enthusiasm and energy rather than wasting time second-guessing his decision and being jealous of my co-worker." —Tracy Johnson, vice president of human resources, Allegis Group

TAKE ONE FOR THE TEAM

Many people dread working in groups. Groups require people to interact differently from what they are used to; people sometimes think teams are a threat to their current position, or they are concerned that teamwork challenges their authority and affects their rank.

Working in groups has many benefits, however. Everyone feels important and included. Ideas and results are often better, because they are shaped by more creativity and opinions. They are argued and discussed from all angles and are more likely to appeal to a diverse audience. Each member of the team can contribute her strengths to the project. When working on a team, it's important to keep the following in mind:

- **Be patient.** Things simply don't get done as quickly in teams, because each step is weighed more carefully, in greater detail, with the opinions of many co-workers.

- **Take other people's ideas and suggestions.** You have to compromise when working in groups. You may think your idea is better, but the majority rules. Don't dwell on it if your ideas are rejected for someone else's, and don't let it spoil your attitude for the remainder of the project. Accept that other people have good ideas, too.

- **Participate actively.** Don't just float by on other team members' work. You are responsible for your fair share.

- **Communicate.** Tell the team leader when you have finished something, as someone else's job may be contingent upon your work. Let the group know if a problem arises and how you intend to handle it.

- **Actively listen.** You must know what is going on for a group to work efficiently. Don't just know your part; know what everyone else is doing, too.

- **Stay organized.** Don't lose all your hard work and efforts because you aren't organized. Keep good tabs on your progress and all the little details like contact information, documents, and schedules.

- **Stay focused on the goals of the group.** It can be easy to lose sight of the team's agenda as you get wrapped up in the details. Remember to keep an eye on the big picture.

ASKING FOR HELP

From time to time, your workload may become overwhelming. Don't be afraid to ask for help. There is a wrong way and a right way to go about this.

- **Explain why you need help.** Maybe there is an overflow from another area, or a project from a different supervisor. Make it clear how long you will need help.

- **Ask a co-worker to take some of your responsibilities.** Just make sure your supervisor approves. She may have another task she would like your co-worker to work on.

- **Don't take on a project you can't handle to begin with.** Speak up immediately and explain what else you are working on. Suggest someone else who would be qualified to handle it, and offer to split the responsibilities. Your supervisor may be able to reassign some of your current tasks, or help you prioritize.

If you consistently need help, the position may not be right for you. It will be hard to admit this to yourself, but you will be much happier in a position that fits your capabilities better. If you've come to this difficult conclusion, talk to your supervisor. It's possible they will train you and help you develop your skills. They might be willing to have a co-worker help you with some of the responsibilities until you can handle them, or hire someone to assist you. You may be given a different position within the organization. In any case, if you do have to leave the company, you are more likely to get a good reference if you are honest and were the one to bring up the problem.

When It's Them

Even if you are on tiptop behavior at all times, your co-workers' behaviors can sometimes present a serious problem. In some cases, it's not you, it's them. It is not enough to polish your own behaviors; you have to learn to deal with the nasty habits of others as well.

GETTING ALONG WITH DIFFICULT CO-WORKERS

Rachel has an amazing ability to control an entire conversation, bouncing from one topic to the next, without allowing a single person to interject. She has to be the center of attention at all times.

Trevor has criticism or feedback on everyone's work. There is not a day that goes by when he does not make a negative comment or "correction" to a co-worker. Nothing is ever done "right," in his opinion.

Bryan is always very nice to your face, but he gossips behind your back. He loves lunchtime conversations and is always in for a great story.

There are all kinds of people with just as many kinds of "issues." The reasons for co-workers' bad behaviors vary widely. Some are insecure, some depressed, some selfish, some mean-spirited, but they are all needy in some way. In essence, people are often difficult to get along with because they are human. Here are some rules of thumb for working with difficult co-workers:

- **Make allowance for co-workers' faults.** This does not mean that you have to accept the effects of their behaviors. It simply means you accept that no one will be perfect and that you yourself are not perfect. Let the little things go and focus on the big issues.

- **Communicate.** Quite often, we don't speak up when someone's behavior is inappropriate, because we are afraid to upset them. Most people would rather dislike a co-worker than be the co-worker who is disliked. Therefore, we remain silent. If you want someone to stop a certain behavior, you must point it out discreetly and privately. Ask them politely to refrain. They may react with surprise and anger, but after the initial shock wears down, their behaviors will cease or lessen and you can continue working side by side.

- **Speak in a professional tone at all times.** Raising your voice will simply aggravate the situation.

- **Don't expect someone to change overnight.** You will surely be disappointed.

- **Forgive and forget.** Don't hold a grudge to all eternity.

- **Be honest with yourself and others.** It doesn't pay to let others continuously get away with murder.

- **Don't rush to judgment.** Make sure there is real impact on the quality of work, not just a personality trait you simply don't like.

- **Kill 'em with kindness.** It never fails.

BEAT A BULLY

Bullying tends to be an accumulation of many seemingly small acts over a period of time. Any of the individual acts may not seem severe, but compiled together they constitute bullying. Bullying behaviors include nitpicking and criticisms of trivial matters. Usually there is a small grain of truth in the criticism, which is why victims ignore the bullying or think they deserve it. Bullying also includes not acknowledging someone personally and professionally. Bullies will often try to single out their victims, not include them, overrule decisions made by their victims, or ignore the victim's suggestions altogether.

You may have been the victim of a bully for so long that you don't even notice it anymore. Don't just accept this kind of behavior. Think of your most difficult co-workers and how they act in the office. If they have one or more of the following characteristics, they may well be a bully: vicious in private, charming in front of others; uses certitude to cover their insecurity; deceptive; controlling; critical of others; impatient, irritable, and aggressive. You may be a victim of a bully if you feel someone steals credit for your work, takes over responsibilities that are yours, sets goals for you to reach that are unobtainable, denies you training, distorts what you say, or shouts at you in front of others.

- **Take action.** You must be direct and firm; don't play the victim. Most bullies will respond better if you confront them yourself. This may be very difficult for the victim of a bully to do, but it is the most effective way to get the behavior to stop.

- **Keep track.** Begin jotting down incidents when you feel you were bullied. Again, each incident may seem trivial on its own, so it is important to have a list of incidents to build context.

- **Face the issue.** Ask the bully if you can speak with them. Be well prepared with what you want to say. Cite the incidents you have jotted down, and ask them to please be more respectful in the future.

Bullies will more than likely deny their behavior, or make excuses, but confronting them usually will put their behavior to a stop, regardless. You have to stand up for yourself. Bullies use subtlety and passive-aggressive behavior to intimidate their victims. When you speak and act directly and assertively rather than shyly and passively, these tactics are ineffective. In some cases, a bully may react to direct confrontation with even more bullying. If their bullying continues, it is time to pull your supervisor into the situation.

DEALING WITH THE DEFENSIVE

People usually act defensively to protect themselves. If you take a step back (figuratively and literally) so they do not feel attacked, it will be much easier to deal with them. People usually are unaware that they are acting defensively.

- **Do not accuse someone of being defensive.** It will make the problem worse. Defensive co-workers are usually trying to cover a perceived failure, so drawing them out will only make them more uncomfortable, and therefore more defensive.

- **Admit your own mistakes.** This will make a defensive person more comfortable admitting theirs. Let them know that you are not perfect and don't expect them to be, either.

- **Focus on the problem, not on the behavior.** If someone is acting defensively because they are insecure about their computer abilities, praise them on their abilities and find a way to make them feel more competent. Ask them a question they are sure to know the answer to.

If you choose to confront them more directly, ask questions rather than make statements, but do not ask direct questions. Say, "It seems like you are upset. Were you offended by something?" instead of "Why are you so angry?" Give the person some time and space. They need time to calm down.

Even though it's an overused cliché, do unto others as you would have done unto you. For as many bad behaviors that exist, there are equally as many bad reactions. No matter what someone has said or done, take some time to think before you act. Consider the most respectful, mature, and professional way to handle the situation. People make mistakes and so do you. It's how you handle them that will set you apart.

CHAPTER SEVEN

. . .

Use 'em or Lose 'em
Make Your Contacts Work for You

"A gossip is someone who talks to you about others, a bore is someone who talks to you about himself, and a brilliant conversationalist is one who talks to you about yourself."

—LISA KIRK,
communications specialist

Whoever said silence is golden wasn't a woman trying to succeed in the job market. Success is not just about *what* you know, it's *who* you know . . . and how you keep it all organized. Make sure you begin building a Personal Dream Team, those people whose helping hands will boost you to the top of the career ladder. With the help of this chapter, you are going to put together a comprehensive and invaluable network of contacts who will become the foundation of your long-term success. You'll learn how to keep up with them and organize them. From people with a heart of gold to those with a pot of gold, the idea is to create a prizewinning database of individuals who know your name and take your calls.

By now, you know the name of the game is *networking*. But all the networking in the world can't help you if you aren't comfortable at events and if you can't find those people's phone numbers and email addresses when you need them. In this chapter, we'll share with you advice on everything from working an event to proper thank-yous and follow-up. We'll also reveal the secret in your files. What files, you ask? You know. Your files. The lists and notes and stacks of business cards containing everything you know about all the contacts you've made throughout your life. The goal is to create a system that allows you to pull up exactly the name you were looking for in a matter of seconds. Read on . . .

Connections for Perfection

EVENTS

Networking events—whether professional, personal, formal, or informal—are great for job-seekers as well as all career women who seek advancement. When planning to attend, there are some simple steps to keep in mind to make your time worthwhile:

- **Arrive early.** For parties, arrive within the first half hour. It's advantageous to go early as it gives you a great opportunity to meet people you don't know as they arrive.

- **Make an entrance.** Keep your head up and make eye contact. If you don't know where you are going, head to the buffet table or bar. This gives you the chance to scout the room, locate someone to speak to, and determine your next movement.

- **Smile as you walk across the room.** Have something in mind to talk about to avoid uncomfortable lulls in conversation. Watch the news before you go, or read a popular book you can discuss. Current events are often icebreakers.

- **Introduce yourself.** Try to give yourself a reference point, such as a mutual friend or acquaintance (Jan's co-worker), so they feel connected to you.

- **Take the initiative to meet people.** This can seem bold and intimidating, but the rules of networking allow you, in fact encourage you, to introduce yourself. Walk up to the person you'd like to meet, say your name, and offer a handshake as you ask what they do.

- **Offer a handshake instead of a kiss.** Extend a handshake when meeting someone for the first time or any time a hand is extended to you. Squeeze firmly but not too firmly, and pump once or twice from the elbow. The handshake should last no more than three seconds. Don't continue to hold the handshake even if the introduction is not complete.

IT WORKS FOR ME

Quick thinking is a virtue

"Coming out of graduate school I interviewed in New York with an Austrian bank for a job that would be located in Vienna, Austria. Two gentlemen conducted the interview: one Austrian, one American. The Austrian spoke fluent English and asked relevant questions during the interview. Of course, 'relevant' in other countries could be considered inappropriate and possibly even illegal in the United States.

"At one point he queried, 'Why aren't you out getting married and having kids right now?' I quickly responded, 'Well, I have a résumé out for that as well.' The American quickly broke into a somewhat restrained laugh, while the Austrian had a quizzical look on his face." —Eileen Creighton, a professional in New York

WORKING THE ROOM

To join in a group conversation, walk up, listen for a few moments, and make a comment that does not change the subject.

If the person you'd like to meet is in the middle of a conversation, don't interrupt. You'll have a chance to speak with the person later.

Once you have the undivided attention of the person you want to network with, don't mistake this as an opportunity to sell yourself to anyone available. No one wants to be bulldozed into giving you a job or business. If you make a hard sales pitch at a networking event, you will be perceived as needy, pushy, inexperienced, and worst of all, desperate.

At a networking event, it's quite possible that someone will ask you, "So, what do you do?" Prepare an answer so this question doesn't catch you off guard. More than likely, however, it will be up to you to bring up the fact that you're searching for a job. It's actually quite easy to broach the subject. Simply ask someone what he or she does, and often they'll return the question and ask what you do. This is your chance to announce that you're looking for a new challenge.

Politely say you'd appreciate it if they could send any contacts or potential leads your way. If they agree, exchange cards or contact information and secure a time to follow-up. After you've handed over your card, leave the topic of job searching. Discussing other topics will help you build a relationship with this individual and allow you to make a lasting, good impression. In general, a networking conversation should last only ten minutes. You want to meet as many contacts as possible, so don't monopolize someone's time, and don't allow yourself to be monopolized.

Avoid alcohol consumption. Getting tipsy is unprofessional, and you lose control of what you say and do. Be aware of your eating and drinking etiquette. Don't stuff yourself before you go, but don't arrive at an event famished either. Clean up after yourself, but don't clear your own plate unless appropriate.

Participate in all activities. You will seem like a team player and a good sport. You'll meet more people if you move around, as you are less approachable when seated. However, know where you are going. Don't just wander aimlessly.

It's rude to leave before all the activities are over, but don't be the last person to leave, unless you're staying to help the host clean up. Take your cue from other guests. Make sure you have talked to everyone you intended to before you leave and say goodbye to the host, any close friends, and contacts you want to keep in touch with.

PITFALLS TO PONDER

Networking's not work

"Women network wrong and treat it like it's a job. They give out business cards. What good is a business card if you haven't established a relationship with someone and they don't remember who you are? If someone can't identify you, then you're not networking. The key is to build a web of contacts who really know you." —Gail Evans, former executive vice president of CNN News Group

BUSINESS CARDS

Passing out your business cards as if they're flyers will ensure that they will be thrown away as if they're flyers. Only pass out cards to those with whom you have had a meaningful conversation, and wait until the end of the exchange.

Even though professional etiquette dictates that it's inappropriate to request a card from someone in a much higher status or position than your own, we say you often have to step out of the comfort zone. If the mood is right, feel free to ask, and couch it by saying that you'll treat the information respectfully. Be clear that you will not share their contact information, nor will you bombard them with calls and emails. If you aren't able to get a card, remember their name and company until you have a chance to write it down. The following day, call the company directory for the person's title, direct line, or email address.

For those who are not of a higher rank or status, be brave enough to offer your card first. You brought these cards for a reason, so use them. Have a pen and paper ready so you can jot down your new contact's information if they don't have cards with them.

- Buy a nice card case, which keeps your cards clean, easy to access, and free of crumples and folds.

- Don't use cards from your previous positions, and don't cross through old information with a pen.

- When someone hands you a card, take a moment to read it. It's rude to put it away without looking at it. Write down any special instructions on the back and store it somewhere safe.

- Do not store others' cards in the same cardholder as your own. You risk giving out valuable contacts' cards to others by mistake.

- Refill your case before all events to ensure you never run out.

- Take any card offered to you. It never pays to be rude when networking.

FOLLOW-UP

So you made some great new contacts at last night's networking party. Follow-up already! If you want to receive calls or emails, then you have to make or send some of your own.

- **Secure follow-up instructions right away.** When you first meet a contact or apply for a position, mention when you will contact them next. Write in your cover letter when you will call. Tell people you have just met when they can expect to hear from you. Ask interviewers when you can reach them.

- **Take any leads a networking contact gives you.** Say your friend gives you a lead for a job you're overqualified for and also doesn't pay enough. Call the job lead anyway. Your friend might find out if you didn't and think you don't appreciate her help. She may think you're not taking her leads seriously, or that you are no longer job searching—which could result in her not giving you leads anymore. Just because you aren't impressed with one job lead doesn't mean you won't be impressed with the next. Make sure you *get* the next one.

- **Contact anyone who serves as a reference for you.** Whether you are offered the position or not, if you want to use them as a reference again you need to keep them informed of your job-search status.

- **The sooner the better.** If someone emails or calls, respond to the message the same day. When you meet someone new, call the next day. If you went to an interview, send a thank-you letter within twenty-four hours, and include instructions as to when you will follow-up on the phone.

THANK-YOU NOTES

Thank-you notes reinforce your interest and qualifications for a job; show you are professional, organized, timely, and appreciative; and offer a chance to demonstrate your communication skills. They provide a great opportunity to convey something you forgot to mention in the initial meeting, and confirm your understanding of topics previously discussed. Fax and email are the quickest methods to send thank-you notes and it can be advantageous to respond quickly, before the position is filled. However, send a handwritten note in the mail as well.

Sending thank-you notes may seem like a no-brainer, but many people forget this important strategy.

- Tailor your thank-you to each individual, although it's acceptable to send a thank-you note to an entire group if a panel of people interviewed you.

- Write in a personal yet professional voice with a positive and confident tone.

- Keep your notes brief and to the point.

- Refer to a specific topic discussed in the meeting so the recipient will easily remember who you are.

- Double-check spelling and grammar.

- If you are sending a thank-you note for the second time, such as after a second interview, it is acceptable to write a briefer note.

Gathering All the Info

A SYSTEM FOR SUCCESS

Keep your active files full of positive contacts. Weed out the ones with less value. Don't throw them away; just file them where they won't keep your active files clogged with inactive information. A good system can help you maximize the effectiveness of past, present, and future relationships, helping you develop and expand a network of contacts, assess who you know now, determine who you want to get to know, and figure out how to meet these people.

Remember high school English class? Can you still recite the five W's that are the necessary components of a good story? Who. What. When. Where. Why. If you don't know them, stop right now and memorize them, because those five words comprise the key to success. If you can pinpoint those facts about everyone you meet, you'll have all the information you need to create a solid Rolodex.® Think of it as writing the story of each person.

> *"I don't remember anybody's name. How do you think*
> *the 'dahling' thing got started?"*
> —ZSA ZSA GABOR

Who?

Get the name of every person you come in contact with. Ask for a card, contact number, or address. Have a place to store the cards you receive and a notebook to jot down the rest of the details. What is their name? Learn how to remember names and faces. Look at their card when you get it. Was there a particular logo or something that tells you more about them? Do they work in the same building as your sister? Anything will help.

One easy tip is to repeat a name as soon as you've been introduced. "Hello, Christine, it's a pleasure to meet you." And say it again several times during the conversation. Studies show that short-term memory is just that—short term. To transfer information into long-term memory, it must be accessed and used. Another tip is to use association. Polly Smith has long blonde hair, just like Molly Sims. Molly—Polly . . . you've got a memory aid to help you recall her name the next time you meet. And don't be shy. If you didn't catch the name, or you forget it right away, ask. We all have memory lapses, and many of us have trouble remembering names. Most people will not be offended at your request. In fact they'll probably be flattered that you cared enough to ask and thankful for the opportunity to ask *your* name again.

PITFALLS TO PONDER

Mind your mouth

"I attended a business conference and impressed a potential client with my product and sales abilities. Later that same evening, I saw her again at a reception, and wanted to introduce my boss to her. Instead of introducing her as Lori, I called her Laura. She simply corrected the error and the conversation went on. I had tried to go out of my way to make her feel important and valued by my company, and calling her by the wrong name, I certainly didn't achieve that. I could have saved myself the embarrassment by taking a moment to double-check the business card she had given me." —Stephanie Jones, a Nebraska-based sales executive

What?

What do they do? Find out what company they work for, where they've worked in the past, and what they consider their expertise. Ask what projects they are currently working on, what associations they belong to, and any other volunteer positions or affiliations they are a part of. What do they do in their spare time? Try to find out what their hobbies and talents are.

Where?

Jot down how you met a person, and who introduced you. Was it at a social function? A business meeting? When you have a reason for contacting them in the future, you'll want this information to make a smooth opening to a conversation or letter. "Hi, Mary, this is Eileen Berner. We met about two months ago at the Little League All-Star game, where your daughter struck mine out! We talked briefly about your company . . ."

If someone else referred them to you, be sure to note that as well. If you met at your children's school, who are her kids? If you were at a cultural event, who was she with? And don't forget that to meet people, you have to *go places*. Sitting at home watching television won't get you any friends other than Monica and Chandler. You can meet people virtually anywhere: school, shopping, class reunions, civic associations, business organizations, through other contacts, cultural affairs, sporting events, the gym, library, volunteering, and political meetings.

When?

When did you meet? You may have known someone for years, but can you really recall when you were introduced to them initially? You can't trust your memory to store a lifetime of encounters, names, dates, preferences, and jobs. Keep an ongoing calendar of all the times you've had lunch, meetings, or other interactions with them.

Why?

Make note of any ideas of how they can help you, and how you can help them. If you attend a networking function, you will come home with dozens of cards and it may be hard to remember which woman you wanted to interview for your next article, so write it down. Why are they a good contact to have? Her usefulness to you may not be obvious now, but someday, somehow, you may need her and her connections. It's like the old adage never to leave bad feelings when you quit a job, you never know when you'll need someone you've bruised. So keep track of even the most peripheral contacts; they might someday be the link you need to the position you want!

PITFALLS TO PONDER

Know your notes

After attending a women's business conference in Manhattan, we received a letter from a public relations company thanking us for our business and reiterating that they would see us in New Orleans in a few weeks—clearly a mistake because we are not one of their clients, and weren't planning a trip to New Orleans. After a good office chuckle, we tossed the letter. To prevent networking events from doing more harm than good, take detailed notes and keep contacts well organized.

CONTACTS, CONTACTS, CONTACTS

Contacts are everywhere. At home, at the office, in the grocery store, at parties and plays and preschool meetings. Teach yourself to be open, to view every person you meet as a potential career resource. No joke. Get friendly with your mechanic, the dry cleaner, the mail carrier. Never say no to a contact! Read the papers and make note of movers and shakers. Check professional publications in your field.

Make business cards your new best friend. Never go anywhere without them. It's a lot easier to ask for a card if you have one to offer in return. And a business card holds a wealth of valuable information—your contact's name, address, phone number, email, and often a company name as well.

If that person mentions other possible contacts, jot that down for future use, too. Places, dates, people or interests in common, put it all in your information system.

Developing Your System

Like a fabulous accessory collection, you've got to have a safe and organized place to put those valuable connections. Decide how you want to organize your files. You may find yourself changing systems as your needs change and grow. When you started out, a simple card file might have served well, but eventually, with hundreds or even thousands of names in dozens of fields, you may need a far more sophisticated system.

Rosanne Badowski worked with legendary General Electric CEO Jack Welch for fifteen years as his executive assistant. In her book *Managing Up: How to Forge an Effective Relationship with Those Above You* (Currency, 2003), she shares her tips to successfully getting organized. "I put technology to my advantage daily. I use an electronic Rolodex® to organize contact information for more than four thousand people. I list lots of little information about each person. This system works for me since it is a quick way to recover data. Use technology to your advantage. Think of the fastest way to retrieve information since there's so much of it. I created a document with keywords that allow me to search for information in several ways, which makes finding names easier and faster."

Create a system that works for you. Find a way to get, and stay, organized. Here are some additional tips for storing your contact information:

- **Don't rely solely on an address book.** Just about everyone has an address book, or notebook, where they can write pertinent information. This is great for writing letters and organizing family contact information, but very cumbersome if you are trying to remember the name of the woman who sat next to you at the professional society luncheon last February. It's a good start, but not necessarily the one to stick with by itself unless you are that rare woman with impeccable handwriting and an ability to organize information.

- **Is it in the cards?** The simplest kind of organizer is the card file. A Rolodex® is an invaluable tool where you can easily access names, phone numbers, email, and addresses. Every great system has its strengths and weaknesses. A Rolodex® keeps your information right at hand and doesn't require an engineer's brain to operate. But a Rolodex® doesn't allow you to easily cross-index or retrieve multiple listings. The same goes for index card files or business card files. Keep your phone organizer handy for easy access, but don't count on it to fill your ultimate networking needs. If you are using a card system, think about color-coding your files: white for business contacts, yellow for personal, pink for social, blue for mentors. And a stick-on dot at the top of each card could further identify it by geography or kind of business.

• **PDA play.** The PDA, or handheld data organizer, is a blessing to today's busy working woman. It can hold notes, lists, addresses, and much more, and it's great for storing data at your fingertips. But, like index cards, it can't do all the juggling and retrieval you will need to maintain a lifetime of networking data. However, remember that many PDAs allow you to transfer data from them into your PC or MAC and vice versa, so time spent entering data is not wasted! Technology is an awesome asset if you're willing to invest the time and money to make it work for you.

• **Computer games.** Our choice for your networking system is your computer. Whether you use a standard database, a spreadsheet, an access program, or a scanner-style system that has the ability to read and extract information from business cards, your computer can store, sort, and retrieve all the data you're able to feed it, and give it back in a format you can easily use to make your networking time efficient. Talk to your favorite computer guru or the helpful tech at your local office or computer store for advice on a specific program to meet your budget and your needs. Don't go too cheap; chances are you'll love the system so much you'll find more and more uses for it, and it's no fun having to set it up all over again later. For that same reason, we advise backing up your database so you never lose it in case of a computer crash. Your contacts are your most important business possession; take care of them and they'll serve you well for years to come.

It may seem tedious to set up a system, but you'll thank yourself over and over as your efforts bear results in the future. Some people use several card files to separate personal from business contacts, or current vs. past vs.

future contacts. Figure out which you make the most use of, those people you think will pave the way to the top for you, and make them your primary file. Highlight them, give them their own section, and find a way to identify and work those contacts.

IT WORKS FOR ME

Be your own private detective

Do you have a phone number jotted down somewhere, but you haven't a clue whose it is or why you have it? Go to Google.com. Type the number, including area code, in the search bar, and, if it's not an unlisted or cell number, you'll get the person's name and address.

ON THE GO BUT IN THE KNOW

Never waste time. Do you commute by plane, train, or bus? Do you take frequent long car trips or spend nights away from home in hotels? You probably find yourself with plenty of wasted time as you wait for people, transportation, or appointments. Use that "sitting down" time to update your files. Other ideal times for catching up are when you're waiting in line at the grocery store or post office, or even if you're early meeting friends for drinks or dinner.

- Sort through cards and make notes of what information you are missing, or what is stale and no longer useful.

- Use your cell phone if the setting is appropriate to keep in touch with casual contacts. Never connect with important business associates this way because it's often distracting to both parties.

- Keep a few notecards or some stationery in your briefcase. Commuting time is terrific for jotting a quick but thoughtful note to say hello to current or potential contacts, customers, clients, or anyone who might be of service to you.

- Make an on-the-go file with the names of all your VIP contacts. Use down time to research ways to make yourself more appealing to them.

QUESTIONS TO ASK YOUR FILES

For every person you add to your filing system, try to include as many of the following descriptions as you can.

1. Name: first, last, title, nickname

2. Physical description and identifying characteristics to help you place her the next time you meet

3. Address: both home and work

4. Phone: work, home, fax, cell

5. Email: work and home

6. Where you met

7. Date you met

8. How you met: introduction, through kids, through a colleague, on the phone

9. What you discussed

10. Name and relationship of the person who introduced you

11. Business or job

12. Geographic location(s)

13. Personal facts: kids, husband or wife, school they attended

14. Friends or colleagues in common

15. What you think this person can do for you

16. What you think you can do for this person

17. Rate this contact for future use, from "not a lot to offer" to "a great new contact"

18. When you should next follow-up with this person

Trying to record all this information on an index card would be impossible. Be sure to leave room for additional categories.

We suggest, if you're investing the time to build a computer database, that you make each contact's information accessible in several ways. You should be able to search by company, by name, by city, by groups, even by key words. That way, you can extract a list without having to read through every file to get your information. Suggested categories would include, but not be limited to:

- First name

- Last name

- Nickname

- City

- State

- Kind of business(es)

- Job(s)

- Hobbies

- Interests

- Business organizations

- Volunteer organizations

- Spouse's name

- Children's names

- Contact

- Who introduced us

This way, if you need to know everyone Mary Jones has introduced you to, it's easy to access. Or if you're flying to New Mexico, you can see at a glance who's there just waiting for your call.

You're not limited to one kind of file. You may opt to choose different ones for different uses. Perhaps you'll want to maintain a Rolodex® for quick access to phone numbers. And an address book in your email program is a must for fast communication.

What should you do with that wealth of business cards you're collecting? If you're transferring the information onto another file system, you can bundle these away or dispose of them. If they're your primary information source, you'll have to organize them in a way that you can get at the information fairly easily. There are all sorts of filing examples— alphabetical, geographical, by business, by type of contact, or perhaps most usefully, by who they are to you. It's a good idea to keep a notebook listing the name and where you have the card filed. This can save valuable time when you're trying to locate a card. But it also lets you see why trying to save information just on business cards can be cumbersome and time-consuming.

Keep It Up to Date

30,000 MILE CHECK

You have your car checked out regularly. You go to the doctor for a physical. Don't forget to do routine maintenance on your information system. Update and correct what you can from your own knowledge— people who've moved or changed jobs or phone numbers. One easy way to help keep your files updated is a simple holiday email. NOT the holiday newsletter filled with news only a family could love, but perhaps a Thanksgiving note adding the sentiment that you are thankful for having them in your life. This is free, quick, and it's a wonderful way to keep track of current email addresses. If it's undeliverable, you'll know in minutes. The better you keep your files maintained, the more you'll be able to draw on them when you need information.

- Check holiday cards for updated addresses.

- Keep an eye on your Caller ID to see if phone numbers have changed.

- Cross-reference your files whenever you get an email from someone. If they're not in your files, get them in there, quick.

- If you gave them your email address, you should certainly be keeping track of theirs.

- If you've divided your contact list into prospects, call the best contacts once a month or so, just to stay in touch and keep your name in front of them.

- Before you call or write to anyone, check your files. Know their name, their spouse's name, their kids, where they work; have it all in front of you. That attention to personal detail is not only flattering, it's very impressive and tells them that you cared enough to listen and remember.

Don't forget about yourself. If you change jobs, phone numbers, or addresses, send out your updated information so you can stay at top of mind.

PUMP IT UP

The more names, the better. The more connections, the better chance you'll have of connecting with career success. But how to gather the right names, the best connections? Try these timely tips:

- **Look closely at your friends, family, colleagues, and neighbors.** Each of them has something to offer you, and you have something to offer them. Success is a two-way street. The more you offer others, the more you are likely to gain in return.

- **Make lists of everyone you know in every aspect of your life.** Start lists of people you don't know very well and who knows them.

Make a list of people you don't know at all and figure out how you can include them in your circle of contacts.

• **Look beyond your circle of friends, acquaintances, and colleagues, too.** Ask people to introduce you to others, and spread your networking web farther afield with each new contact. If you see an article about the CEO of a company in your field, and you know she went to school with a friend of yours, call your pal and ask for an introduction. Explain what you're doing and how she's an important part of your vision for success. You just have to ask.

• **Take advantage of outplacement services.** If you were laid off and offered outplacement services, jump at the chance for this coaching. Get to know the principals by name and make your presence known in their offices. More times than not, they won't seek you out or extend a helping hand without your enthusiastic participation.

• **Make a wish list of people you'd like to meet but never really expect to.** If you don't reach for the stars, you won't ever get them. Even if it seems there's no way you'll ever meet Bill Gates or Madonna, if you look for ways to get nearer to them, who knows what fascinating and helpful people you might meet along the way?

• **Join, join, join.** Where could you find a better list of contacts than in the membership directory of your professional association? People who join these groups expect to be contacted, so don't let them down. Plus, if you get active in community affairs, your face and your name will become familiar to others and keep you at the top of their list when opportunities to help you arise. The relationships you cement will be well worth the investment of time and effort.

• **Make organizations pay off.** Meet and greet everyone you see. Don't sit in a corner and expect others to come to you.

• **Learn to be assertive.** Not aggressive, assertive. Pick up the phone and call someone you don't know, write a letter, send an email.

- **Always follow-up with a new contact.** A phone call, an email or a note will reinforce your image in that person's mind, increasing the likelihood of name recognition the next time you meet or contact her.

- **Be the first to make networking work.** Find a way to help a new contact. Send an article you think she'd enjoy, or refer her business to someone else. Your interest in others will come back tenfold as renewed interest in you.

IT WORKS FOR ME

Share your knowledge

"Women must share information and advice with other women. It makes all of us even smarter. For example, how do you know how much money to ask for if you don't ask other women? Most women tend to make up these rules about what's right and wrong in business and the workplace and it's crazy. For example, she thinks, 'I can't ask a friend to introduce me to her father who might be a prospective client because she's my friend.' I say that's nonsense!"
—Gail Evans, author of *She Wins, You Win: A Guidebook for Making Women More Powerful* (Gotham Books, 2003)

- **Work hard on making a good impression.** A firm handshake, eye contact, a smile and pleasant conversation will add a contact to your files in a heartbeat. A favorable impression will work in your favor when you ask for help later.

- **Start an Internet newsletter.** Find a topic you're an expert on, or make yourself an expert in a particular area. It can be anything from community news to time-saving tips for busy career people. Keep it light and readable. Send it to everyone appropriate on your contact list, and include a request to people to pass it on if they enjoyed it. Also include an email address for a subscription. You may get a few new names, or you may be inundated. In fact, you may end up as a newsletter publisher! In any event, you'll be expanding the number of people who know about you, and whom you know about.

IT WORKS FOR ME

Know where to network

Adina Mangini, a human resources professional for GlaxoSmith-Kline, says, "Fifty-four percent of GlaxoSmithKline's salespeople come from networking referrals. There are nearly seven thousand GSK employees across the United States. Find someone you know to get your foot in the door, and if you don't know anyone, go to your doctor—for a checkup and a few good leads. More often than not, your doctor's sales rep will be willing to refer you because an important client recommended you."

REACH OUT AND TOUCH SOMEONE

Now that you've learned how to build and maintain a network of names, don't just sit there admiring your list. Use it, and make it work for you. Stay in touch. Since you never know who's going to be holding your golden ticket to success, you don't want to overlook a single prospect, hot or not.

- Use email to stay in touch. Don't be a pest, but an occasional cheery note, or a forwarded article you think will be of interest will keep their interest alive, too.

- Use email to send a brief note shortly after meeting a new contact. Follow up two to three weeks later, just to stay in touch. Ask a pertinent question to elicit a response, or invite the contact to meet for drinks or lunch.

PITFALLS TO PONDER

Pregnant or plump?

"At a business meeting, I asked a colleague I hadn't seen in a long while when she was due. 'Actually, I had a baby girl eight months ago,' she responded. I quickly apologized and congratulated her, but I haven't been comfortable around her since. It dawned on me that I hadn't spoken to her in almost two years. Had I kept in touch every so often, I would have known she was pregnant, sent a card when she had the baby, and wouldn't have stuck my foot in my mouth and damaged an important networking relationship." —Embarrassed in Arizona

THE MORE YOU GIVE, THE MORE YOU GET

It's not just about contacts. It's about relationships. And one way to so-lidify relationships is with consideration. Remember, it's often the little things that count such as cards, gifts, a phone call, an interesting article clipped from the paper. Here are some hints on inexpensive ways to keep yourself in their minds.

- **Meet for drinks and appetizers.** This is an easy way to say hello and spend a few minutes with a casual contact. Invite a contact to lunch. If there's someone she knows who you want to know, too, ask her to bring that person along, you're treating. Tell her why, of course. Nobody likes to feel like they're being used without their permission.

- **Make a sports date.** This is a classic stay-in-touch ploy in the world of men. It's time women adopted it, too. There are so many avenues to pursue—golf, tennis, jogging, walking, a Pilates class, aerobics, kickboxing. You'll be doing your heart a favor as you work on your networking, too!

- **Have a networking party.** Like a Tupperware party, but you're selling yourself, not plastics. Invite a group you think would be congenial for brunch or wine and cheese. No need to do any kind of presentation, you're just inviting folks to get together socially, but your hostessing skills and your enthusiasm will leave them with a positive impression. Make it a tradition. Make your get-togethers so great people will be clamoring to get in. Remember reading about the grand salons in Paris? They were *the* place to see and be seen.

IT WORKS FOR ME

Who you know helps more than you know

Maureen Kelleher, director of experienced recruiting for accounting giant Ernst & Young, says internal referrals get more attention than people who don't put their network to work. "It demonstrates creativity and relationship building. I like to see potential applicants follow the right protocol of applying online. But to get the attention of a recruiter, go through your background and figure out who you know at the organization of your choice or within the profession. Even if you're a star accountant, you might not know someone at Ernst & Young, but you could very well know someone at Pricewaterhouse-Coopers, and they might know someone at E & Y to connect you with. Follow the trail from your contact to the recruiter responsible for this position. Let your contact know you'd like the benefit of their advice and insight on the role, division, and company. You won't necessarily get the job because you know someone, but you have a much better chance of being heard."

Don't forget gifts and cards, either. They needn't be expensive, just appropriate to the occasion and the relationship. In fact, elaborate and ostentatious gifts can often be seen as inappropriate and could do you more harm than good. Keep it simple, tasteful, and don't forget that a touch of humor or a special sentiment can make her day by making her smile! In co-author

Robyn Spizman's book *The GIFTionary: An A-to-Z Reference Guide for Solving Your Gift-Giving Dilemmas . . . Forever!* (St. Martin's Press, 2003), she offers many suggestions that encourage adding pizzazz to your gifts. The key is not to spend a great deal, but to add your presence to the present.

- Send cards for appropriate occasions . . . birthday, anniversary, new job, promotion, get well, congratulations on the new car, the new pet, the new mate!

- Drop a note to say "well done."

- Clip an article you think she'll enjoy, or send a special recipe for something she admired at your home.

REACH FOR THE STARS

You're almost there. You've developed a knockout information system, you're keeping it updated, you're staying in touch. Now what? It's time to put those connections to use, to help you reach those unreachable stellar individuals who can really put your career path on the high road to success. But how? You've got your Personal Dream Team—your list of those in high and low places who you dream might help you on your way to the top. Now start to make that dream come true.

 IT WORKS FOR ME ·

Know how to network

"Publishing is a small business," says Lynette Harrison, Publisher of *InStyle* magazine. "People move from magazine to magazine, and we all know each other. Look at the masthead of a magazine for people to contact and ask for an informational interview. Even if there is not an opening at that magazine, chances are someone will know someone at another magazine where there is an opening. When you are trying to get someone's attention, learn everything you can about that person. Do the research and be prepared with three questions that prove you've done some homework."

- **Choose your target.** Is there someone in your profession, one special someone, who holds all the keys? Find out all you can about him or her. That includes likes, dislikes, school and professional affiliations, all the things you've used to develop your files.

- **Check your files.** Look for any connection: a friend, a friend of a friend, a business contact of a friend of a friend. Don't be afraid to ask for an introduction. In fact, banish the words *fear* and *afraid* from your vocabulary. You're on the way to the top, and there's no room on this road for timidity.

- **If you can't find a connection, make one.** Volunteer to work the check-in table at a business conference you know she'll be attending. Offer to interview her for a company publication. Find something you have in common, such as love of opera. Write and ask if you might have a few minutes of her time for a phone call. Tell her why, briefly, and suggest a date and time. If she doesn't answer, follow up in about ten days. If she's written a book, ask if you might take her to lunch to discuss it, or if you might make an appointment to have her sign it. Be bold, go after what you want, but don't be pushy, aggressive, or obnoxious. Be sure to follow up with a thank-you, no matter how you've been treated.

Make a habit of reading the executive announcements and awards section of industry publications. When you see the mention of someone you'd like to meet, clip the article and send it to him or her with a note of congratulations, including why you'd like to meet.

IT WORKS FOR ME

Nab a number

"A phone call gets my attention. I know it's difficult to obtain a name and number from a large company, so that's exactly why I'm impressed when someone is able to track me down. The conversation should be short and friendly—just enough so that I can form an impression about your personality. Periodic contact is also valuable. It demonstrates a sincere and strong interest in what I have to offer." —Wendy Smith, a human resources professional at Texas Instruments

Networking is the cornerstone of your career. This is true at all levels and in all lines of work—from the entry-level college grad who's looking to land her first job to the entrepreneur who's branching out on her own to the corporate bigwig who continues to advance. It's a constant learning process and an ever-evolving sport as you meet new people and juggle even more contacts. An appreciation for the value of networking and the need to maintain a system for your contacts will benefit your career throughout its many phases.

CHAPTER EIGHT

Be a Pro in Motion
Learn to Sell Yourself with Sizzle

"A strong, positive self-image is the best possible preparation for success."
—DR. JOYCE BROTHERS,
celebrity psychologist

Why is it when a man lets the world know how great he is, he is labeled confident, but when a woman does the same thing, she's called conceited, arrogant—or even worse?

Many of us were taught at an early age not to brag or boast. We also learned quickly that other people rarely enjoy the company of braggarts. However, there's a clear distinction between a woman who is so full of herself that she doesn't even notice other people and someone who is passionately confident about her success. This isn't about self-*absorption*. It's about self-*promotion*. If you don't share what you've accomplished and learn to be your own best promoter, how will others know your capabilities? If you don't promote yourself, who will?

Savvy women know how to promote themselves. Dr. Phil would be proud of them—they're not afraid to tell it like it is. That said, self-promotion doesn't come easy for everyone and you may be one of the many women who finds it difficult.

Some women perceive success as a sequence of events or even chance, such as being in the right place at the right time. Others believe that if you do a job well, the recognition will follow. Both of these viewpoints are misguided. We've all seen people receive a promotion when everyone knows management passed over a more qualified candidate. If you aren't out there tooting your own horn and promoting your accomplishments, they may very well go unnoticed. Even though nothing's ever guaranteed, promoting yourself helps protect you from layoffs, since your boss is unlikely to fire the highest flier. And, your visibility is excellent fuel for when you ask for a raise at your next evaluation.

 IT WORKS FOR ME ··

Just say it!

"Most men will come out and say, 'I am a solid tennis player' or 'I am great with numbers.' You should feel free to say these things, too. When people hear statements of confidence even if they are self-made, they tend to believe them. And while at the end of the day, the proof is in the pudding, the propellant is in the promoting. Claim your area of expertise so that you have the chance to prove it." —Branding specialist Samantha Ettus, president, Ettus Media Management in New York

Warming Up Your Vocal Chords

You have to make a conscious decision to become a pro at promoting yourself. If you're too reserved about your own successes, are you going to be able to promote your clients, work, or the products you sell? How about the successes of others on your team? You need to work hard, but you also need to be able to broadcast your success to others. Let's face it. No amount of self-promotion will make a difference if you can't deliver the goods. You have to be able to perform, but don't think you have to have increased the company's cash flow by 20 percent to make this happen.

It's all about understanding your strengths and then expressing them in the best possible manner.

START WITH YOURSELF

> *"Don't compromise yourself. You are all you've got."*
> — JANIS JOPLIN

Before you can convince anyone else of your worth, you have to be convinced of it yourself. If you don't take your self-worth seriously, now's the time to get to work on your self-esteem. Here are a few tips on learning to love yourself:

- **Look at yourself positively.** Rather than finding things to criticize, find things to compliment.

- **Never put yourself down, either privately or publicly.** A little self-deprecation is often fun and ok. But you're your own best friend, and it's important not to beat up on yourself.

- **Be realistic about your flaws.** Take steps to correct them as we've outlined in chapters 2 and 3, but don't let them grow into a mountain from the tiny molehill they are in reality.

- **Learn from other people's criticisms.** Grow positively from them, but don't grow more timid. Always consider the source: Is the criticism coming from someone who has your best interests at heart, or from someone who merely wants to tear you down?

- **Celebrate your successes.** Reread your professional portfolio to bolster your image of the successful you.

- **Spend your time with people who make you feel good.** Everyone needs a cheering squad or fan club. Celebrate those people in your life and allow them to celebrate you.

- **Learn to laugh.** Humor is a wonderful pick-me-up, and the world loves a happy person.

- **Keep it in perspective.** When you feel lowest, look at others and realize they have the same self-doubts and fears you do. If they can beat their demons, you can beat yours, too.

- **We're all human.** Look at someone successful and say, "He puts his pants on one leg at a time, the same as I do." Adopt that theme for yourself. Whomever you admire, she's human, just like you are, and with the same portion of strengths, weaknesses, fears, talents. She's learned to use all her traits to her advantage, just like you can. She puts her stilettos on one at a time.

- **Be yourself.** If you keep trying to be someone else, you're doomed to fail. Glorify yourself and be the most and the best you can be. Trying to be someone else will lead you to frustration and failure. You deserve to be the best *you*, not the second-best *her*.

IT WORKS FOR ME

Career coaching on the cheap

No dough? Career coaching doesn't have to be an expensive investment. Just head to the nearest video store to rent these movies for hours of inspiration and positive energy.

- **Erin Brockovich.** A poor mother of two forces her way into a legal assistant position in an office of co-workers determined to oust her. Taking on a huge case, she triumphs through hard work and an undefeatable spirit. Lesson Learned: Don't sit back and hope for what you want. When the going gets tough, the tough get going.

- **Legally Blonde 2: Red, White, and Blonde.** Elle Woods storms the White House as an animal rights activist, letting her heart guide her to the top, not underhanded politicians. Lesson Learned: Do it your own way. Don't compromise who you are, but find a way to succeed and still be true to yourself.

- **Dangerous Minds.** From the Marines to an inner-city classroom, Michelle Pfeiffer fearlessly adjusts her approach to success. Lesson Learned: Don't let fear stop you from giving your all. Bravery will persevere, and if one way doesn't work, try another.

Create Your Sales Pitch

Of course everybody needs to know how terrific you are, but there are some specific people you must not neglect. For instance, your boss may think you hung the moon, but what if he or she leaves the department or the company? There goes your booster club. You never want to depend on just one person. Make sure the whole chain of command is aware of you and your talents and accomplishments. Be prepared for opportunities to promote yourself.

- **Your elevator speech.** The one-minute impression you make must be brief and to the point. You don't want to give them your whole life story, just tell them who you are and what you do in a minute or less. Keep it very brief. You should be able to get through your entire pitch while you make a cup of coffee, reload paper into the printer, or get through the lunch line.

- **Get the basics down pat.** Become an articulate speaker. To test your speaking abilities—not just in front of large groups, but everyday conversation as well—record yourself with a tape recorder. Even though none of us love how we sound, you should be able to identify flaws in your speech pattern. If this is difficult, consider joining Toastmasters or investing in a voice coach to teach you breathing techniques, voice modulation, speaking in a pleasing rhythm, and how to use your voice to emphasize important points. A coach can also give you hints on body language and vocabulary to help you make the most of your vocal contacts.

- **Think of your goal.** Think of *why* you want to make a good impression. Focus on the job, the house, the future you want, not the immediate fear of not pleasing those in front of you.

- **Practice your poker face.** Remember that others can't tell how you feel inside unless you let them know. Concentrate on appearing confident and upbeat, and chances are you'll make everyone think you are.

- **Display yourself as you would a treasured keepsake.** Others see the outward "you," the clothes, manners, attitudes, language, expressions, and gestures. Make them positive and appealing and the world will see you as you want to be seen.

FINDING THE WORDS

When you are promoting yourself, it's all about what you bring to the table. Nobody cares if you were an account executive or VP of Operations. But they would be impressed if you continuously exceeded your quotas or were recognized with honors and awards for being an exceptional employee.

- Don't ever lie.

- Select a few quantifiable and qualifiable accomplishments about yourself to highlight when talking.

- Use strong active verbs and adjectives to make a point. Use persuasive talking to get your message across.

We call it Promotion 101, and there is a right way to share your accomplishments so it doesn't sound merely like empty bragging. There are words you can use that add credibility to your message. Choose words from this list to develop meaningful statements about your accomplishments:

I accelerated . . .

I championed . . .

I executed . . .

I facilitated . . .

I generated . . .

I enhanced . . .

I expanded . . .

I implemented . . .

I increased . . .

I initiated . . .

Here are some other words to choose from and practice with: **A**ccelerate, achieve, adapt, advise, analyze, **B**udget, build, **C**hampion, coach, collaborate, complete, conduct, coordinate, create, cultivate, **D**esign, develop, devise, direct, double, **E**liminate, encourage, enhance, establish, evaluate, execute, expand, **F**acilitate, foster, found, **G**enerate, **H**andle, head, **I**dentify, implement, improve, increase, influence, initiate, instruct, integrate, interpret, invent, **L**aunch, lead, leverage, **M**aintain, manage, mediate, mentor, **N**avigate, negotiate, nurture, **O**bserve, obtain, orchestrate, organize, orient, **P**artner, persuade, plan, present, produce, publish, **Q**uadruple, **R**educe, refine, reorganize, research, **S**olve, strategize, streamline, supervise, **T**ailor, target, triple, **U**pdate, upgrade.

MEASURABLE RESULTS

"My grandfather once told me that there were two kinds of people: those who do the work and those who take the credit. He told me to try to be in the first group; there was much less competition."

—INDIRA GANDHI,

Prime Minister of India from 1966–84

Think about measurable results. A CEO is measured by her company's success, a retailer by the bottom line, a teacher by her students' growth and knowledge, and an athlete by her stats. How can you establish measurable results to help others see your successes? How can you make sure a team's successes reflect on you?

- **Set a bottom line to measure from.** Sales numbers, quality of work, or whatever is most applicable to your line of work—it has to be something you can control, or it will be of no use to you. For example, stock price won't work because that is controlled by too many influences. Think of numbers of customers, percentage increase in sales, repeat business, efficiency, productivity of employees, complaints, or speed of service.

- **Measure yourself.** Not just from where you start but by where you want to end up. Excellent ratings on your performance review, 100 percent on testing; percentage of customers helped in a timely fashion or reordering with larger orders.

- **Make goals achievable but not easy.** You're much more impressive when you show you can stretch yourself and your associates to achieve the company's goals.

- **Improve morale—yours and others.** Make a happy workplace one of your goals, and work hard to achieve it. Satisfied employees are more productive and accurate, and your effort to improve the atmosphere will be a feather in your career cap.

- **Be a cheerleader for the company and for yourself.** If you're seen as a strong advocate internally for the company's policies, products, and services, then you're likely to be selected as a representative for external events. This can include press interviews, speaking engagements, and other special functions. All of this serves to promote your career success.

Just Okay Self-Promotion: "The hospital administrators were so excited that they now have a fully stocked toy room for their juvenile patients. You should have seen those little kids' faces light up when they first got their hands on the brand-new dolls, trains, and books the auxiliary donated."

Awesome Self-Promotion: "I chaired a committee that successfully raised $10,000 to buy toys for the hospital. For the past three years the hospital had tried to do this unsuccessfully, so I took the initiative to establish a designated toy fund through the families of patients at the hospital. You should have seen those little kids' faces light up when they got their hands on the brand-new stuff."

Just Okay Self-Promotion: "I helped to significantly exceed my sales quota last year. It was the first time in history our division had such an increase."

Awesome Self-Promotion: "At the annual meeting, the chairman of the board announced that the company's bottom-line profit increase was entirely due to the 200 percent sales increase in my division last year. He even congratulated me by name in front of our stockholders as a terrific leader."

Just Okay Self-Promotion: "Note to Management: I'd like to commend my department for the seamless switchover in computer systems. We managed to get the job done under budget, with no major foul-ups, and we've developed a system that will serve us well for years to come. It was a pleasure to direct this talented, dedicated group."

Awesome Self-Promotion: "Note to Management: I'd like to thank you for the opportunity you gave me to lead the development and execution of this incredible new state-of-the-art tracking system. I'm proud management invested time and trust in me to spearhead a program that will benefit us through cost-effectiveness, efficiency, and improved customer satisfaction. My team worked together superbly, and this is a shining accomplishment for our organization."

POSITIVELY POSITIVE THINKING

How you speak often defines how others view you. The more positive you are, the more impressed they will be. Never say "I hope" when you can say "I know." "I know" defines you not only as positive, but as the expert, too. When you say "I know," others are going to take you at your word. When you say "I hope," they're liable to think you are weak or wishy-washy. Example: "I hope you find the project results satisfactory. We really worked hard on them." That's not nearly as strong as you want it to be. You want to come out swinging: "I know you're going to be thrilled with the project results. We did everything possible to make it a success and we really hit a home run." In other words, put them on your team as soon as you open your mouth. You'll look and sound more confident, and that's how you will be perceived and treated, too.

- **Try not to use "I" excessively when talking about your accomplishments.** Instead, hype your accomplishments and successes. If you can make your story sound exciting, others will want to hear it. Think of it this way: Nobody wants to hear about how some fellow climbed a mountain and how great that made him, but if he can tell them about the mountain, its challenges and beauties, and how splendid the view was from the top, he'll hold their attention and gain their admiration. Use that for yourself. Don't repeat endlessly how smart, talented, and accomplished you are. Let your story illustrate that for you, as you describe the results. Not only will this amaze people with your abilities, it will shape their image of you, too, without the drawbacks of jealousy.

- **Shower third parties with your successes.** If you've won an award, issue a press release. Send it to local papers and industry publications. When it's printed, clip it and send out the article to your contact list. After all, the papers thought well enough of you to publicize your accomplishment, the least you can do is help spread the word.

- **Attach your contacts to your success.** If others think you're calling, emailing, or making appointments just to brag, they'll resent the wasted time. If they think you're concerned about them or attracted to them, they're likely to be more willing to spend time with you. Forget, "Hi, Mrs. Jones. Just wanted to fill you in on what's been happening with me. I was appointed to the Blue Ribbon Commission last week, and this week I got my name in the paper as one of the rising young stars in the industry." Who cares? But if you approach her like this, "Mrs. Jones, I am so excited to tell you that your name came up at the Blue Ribbon Commission meeting last week. The commissioner thinks you'd be a great asset as an advisor to my committee, and I agree. Can I invite you to lunch to discuss the project?" you'll grab her attention, stroke her ego, and make her want to hear more.

- **Thank your boss for your success.** Instead of always focusing on your successes when talking to your boss, make her feel good about how she's contributed to them. Don't say, "I've been chosen to represent our company in the United Way campaign this year." Instead tell her, "Thanks to your guidance, I've enhanced my ability to ask the right questions and generate cooperation among groups. I know that's what led to my being named to the United Way board this year. I appreciate your mentoring."

- **Target your audience.** Don't bore someone with a list of your honors if it has no relevance to their interests. Figure out ahead of time what tickles their fancy, and play to it. If you're talking to volunteers, emphasize how well you've worked with charity groups or in raising funds for their projects. If it's business professionals, talk about the articles you've written and achievements you've made in an area of interest to them.

- **Attend workshops and seminars.** Be vocal, speak up, but only when you have something constructive to add to the conversation.

- **Volunteer at work.** Serve on committees, public outreach initiatives, or planning sessions. Such positions will help promote your career.

 IT WORKS FOR ME ··

Lead that association

"There are always excuses for how we as women, especially students or engineers, don't get the opportunity to demonstrate what we can do or aren't given the chance to learn," says Irene Chang, a chemical engineer at ExxonMobil. She credits the Society of Women Engineers for opening many doors for her. You can seek out similar opportunities through volunteer or elected positions in industry organizations in your field. "My participation in SWE gave me several opportunities to take on large responsibilities, lead groups of people in challenging teams, accomplish more than the ambitious goals we set," says Chang, "and all without the fear or pressure of long-lasting career implications!"

- **Speak at local functions such as League of Women Voters debates, church events, and school meetings.** Offer to introduce other speakers, even if it's just for the experience of speaking in public.

- **Get yourself elected or appointed to boards, commissions, and public agencies.** Such positions provide terrific opportunity for promoting your career strengths and your personal passions. They may also afford the chance to be in the local news.

- **Write letters to the editor.** Make sure they are written in flawless English, with correct spelling and grammar, and that they state your point strongly and succinctly.

- **Be modest, but not too modest.** When others want to give you credit, take it. Never say, "No, it was nothing," when someone compliments you. If they thought enough of you to compliment you, accept graciously.

- **Don't wait for opportunities to come to you.** Ask for extra assignments. Your successful work speaks volumes about your drive, enthusiasm, and devotion to your company. It will be noticed and rewarded.

IT WORKS FOR ME

Pointers from a PR pro

When it comes to selling yourself, who knows better than PR professionals? Kristen Lewis, who nabbed her dream job as a publicist for a book publisher, says, "Knowing even the basics of PR 101 can go a long way in career advancement. *You* are the product in your career. You have to keep *you* 'top of mind' with potential or current employers, just like you would with whatever you are promoting to the news media.

"When I interviewed for my position, I had to select a book from our spring catalog to develop a pitch for, and I chose one that hadn't even been published yet. All I had to go on was a cover design and summary description of the book, *Sixty Million Frenchmen Can't Be Wrong: Why We Love France & Not the French* (Sourcebooks Trade, 2003). I chose it on the basis that the morning I got the assignment, the very first negative headlines came out bashing the French for not jumping on the Iraqi war bandwagon. I used this as my peg for a media pitch sent, ironically, on Valentine's Day (L'amour No More for the French—with French chocolates) which was hand-delivered to my publisher. I followed it up with faxes to her of all the anti-French articles that came out in the days that followed, showing that I picked up on this media nerve from the get-go (and simultaneously keeping my name in front of her). I got the job."

WORK THE WEB

You're educated and you're an expert in your field. You've got a solid list of email contacts. Start a website. Domain names are relatively inexpensive, and you can find someone to design a web page if you can't do it yourself. You'll have to do a little work to get your site included in the major search engines, but the exposure and "hits" will be great promotion for your expertise. Just be sure you do it right and keep it updated. After all, it's a direct reflection of you.

Let other Internet users help you achieve your goals. Join Usenet discussion groups in your field of interest. You can learn a lot in these groups, and you may make some very useful contacts. Be careful of giving out personal information. You might consider a separate screen name just for use in public forums on the Net.

DO'S AND DON'TS AS YOU TOOT YOUR HORN

- Don't expect people to know what you want if you haven't told them. They aren't mind readers.

- Do learn to cope gracefully with disappointment. Your goals will not be everybody's, and not everyone will respond to your self-promotion efforts. Learn to shrug your shoulders and move on to the next target.

- Don't ever denigrate yourself. If you can't be positive, be silent.

- Do make a self-promotion calendar. Mark contact birthdays, anniversaries, and other important dates. Note deadlines for publications, and each month list a number of people to be contacted in the next 30 days. Make sure no month goes by without a drive to let others know something about you—and how this information can support them.

- Do give credit where credit is due. Others will appreciate your praise, and will likely return the favor.

- Don't ever step on toes. You can't afford to make enemies, even if they are horrible people who deserve it. You never know when you might need them in the future, and you don't want to have bad vibes with other people in your community or industry.

Just as networking in the previous chapter is essential for career advancement, so too is the ability to confidently sell yourself. In addition to knowing your strengths and keeping track of your successes, never lose sight of the fact that you've got to be your own best promoter. Don't rely on others to toot your horn.

CHAPTER NINE

Cope with Curveballs by Swinging Back
Don't Let Life's Challenges
Derail Your Career

"I have always grown from my problems and challenges, from the things that don't work out, that's when I've really learned."

—CAROL BURNETT

Laid-off, downsized, divorced, and rejected. Those are just some of the curveballs life throws our way. We all face unforeseen challenges that we wish we could avoid, but it's imperative not to let them derail your career. When they are aimed at you, it takes a resilient woman to dodge them artfully and move on. The worst reaction is one in which we consider ourselves victims and we become paralyzed by these obstacles. In addition to using these issues as learning experiences, we'll offer proactive advice to not only cope with the hand we've been dealt but to thrive in spite of it.

 **IT WORKS FOR ME** ··

Dare to dazzle

"Realizing that you can't control the exact outcome of life does not need to translate into resignation. To the contrary, it can inspire valiant action. It frees you to play fearlessly to create an extraordinary future, without dwelling on the crisis du jour or lamenting about how life might actually turn out. What you say is possible and not possible, coupled with how you react to the events that occur in your life, determines your future. It all comes down to what you proclaim to be within your realm of possibility. Dare yourself to be dazzling." —Kirsten Osolind, founder of reinventioninc.com, an online brand and image consultancy

The Curveballs

You are not alone. More than likely, what is happening to you has happened to thousands of other professionals before you. Every personal problem is surmountable, and it doesn't have to destroy your career.

DOWN IN THE DUMPS

Depression is a disease that affects one in four people. It is not always just a feeling or emotion, and it won't necessarily go away. People who suffer from depression often don't understand the disease and consider it a sign of personal laziness, weakness, or lack of motivation. Many people don't realize they are depressed. Common signs of depression:

- Feeling blue for days or weeks at a time
- Change in sleep habits
- Weight gain or loss
- Anxiety attacks
- Lack of energy
- Decrease in sex drive
- Alienating yourself from friends and family
- Increased drug or alcohol use

- Questioning your religion or other personal values

- Thoughts of suicide

IT WORKS FOR ME

Don't let despair hold you down

"Some battles may not come out the way you'd hoped, but don't back away. If you feel despair, take the moment and feel despair. But then press on. If you persevere and see it through to the end, you'll get results. You have to develop this habit, even when you don't want to, because it will always be easier to give up." —Erin Brockovich

Everyone feels depressed on occasion, but it should go away within a day or two. If it does not, there are several things you can do to fight it. In addition to seeking advice and treatment from your doctor, here is some advice to beat the blahs:

- Take time to relax every day.

- Talk to your support network of friends and family about how you are feeling.

- Start an exercise routine, but not an overly aggressive one.

- Maintain a regular life routine. Get up at the same time every day and go to bed at the same time.

- Get involved in your community. Join a group such as a choir or social club.

- Consider counseling services or a group therapy session.

Depression can easily affect your work habits and your job can quickly start to feel overwhelming. You may not be able to take pride in it, or feel like you can give your best effort. It is important not to let your work performance decrease, though. Losing your job and dealing with economic problems will certainly not make you feel any better.

- Consider coming in early, or staying a little later so you do not feel rushed and will have time to take breaks during the day.

- Try to meet deadlines ahead of time so you can avoid stress.

- Try not to take on overwhelming projects that will consume too much of your time. Delegate work whenever possible.

- Take on a small project that you know you can do well. The satisfaction and kudos from your manager will give you a little boost.

- Stay organized. Keep your workspace clean. Bring in personal items for your desk.

- Read through emails, thank-you notes, good performance reviews, and other positive letters. Dwell on previous work successes to make you feel more inspired about your job.

- Take time to get up and stretch. Go outside for lunch and breaks, or keep a window open for fresh air.

- Talk to your co-workers. Do not isolate yourself.

DEALING WITH DIVORCE

Just because statistics show that half the marriages in this country end in divorce doesn't make you feel any less alone. Share your news, but refrain from wearing your bitterness or betrayal on your sleeve in the workplace. Usually the demands of co-workers and supervisors are the last things you want to deal with during or immediately following a divorce. But, getting back to work can boost your self-esteem, put your mind on other things, and bring home a paycheck to avoid financial stress. It can also provide a chance to socialize. Most importantly, your career can provide you with a sense of stability and accomplishment to combat the sense of failure many women feel after a divorce.

BOOK BREAK

Motivational speaker and self-proclaimed actionist Jessica Weiner tackles her own body image issues and delivers a powerful philosophy of loving your whole self unconditionally, regardless of your size. *A Very Hungry Girl: How I Filled Up on Life . . . And How You Can, Too!* (Hay House, 2003) offers ways to combat negative feelings and fulfill your potential by understanding the experiences of other women.

No matter what you're feeling or the circumstances surrounding your divorce, it's essential not to allow this personal crisis to diminish your professional worth. Since divorce can be an all-encompassing experience, it's often next to impossible to separate personal and professional feelings. Yet the fact remains that the failure of your relationship doesn't lessen your value in the workplace.

As you divvy your tangible possessions, do not dispose of your professional confidence. Now is when you need it most.

BEAT THE BIOLOGICAL CLOCK

Many women put off starting or expanding their families in favor of pursuing career goals. Sometimes this proves satisfying both personally and professionally. Other times there's a hefty price to pay: an inability to conceive when the moment seems right. While this is an extraordinarily personal decision, the truth is that you can almost always get a job or advance your career, but you can't always have a baby.

Since fertility in women diminishes by 50 percent by age thirty-five, Dr. Carlene Elsner, a reproductive endocrinologist in Atlanta, suggests not wasting precious time if having a baby is indeed your priority. "If you're actively trying to conceive for three to six months without success, consult a reproductive endocrinologist." By working with your doctor or other medical professionals, you can explore a wide range of options for expanding your family.

CREDIT CHECKS

Many employers will check your credit rating as part of the interview process. Excessive debt or poor credit history is often a rationale for rejecting a potential candidate for a job or promotion. Some of the common positions and responsibilities where a credit check may be warranted:

- Retail sales professionals who have access to cash and merchandise.

- Payroll and accounting professionals who have access to a company's accounts and spending authorization.

- Bank and financial services employees with access to money and confidential information about clients.

- Scientists, security personnel, government employees, and top executives with access to classified files and other confidential and sensitive information.

- Professionals with key decision-making or spending authority, including those who frequently work with outside constituents and may be susceptible to potential bribes.

The main reason employers want to check your credit history is to rule out any potential for conflict with someone who is deeply in debt and may be tempted to steal money, merchandise, trade secrets, or consumers' identifications. Some employers believe that a poor credit history hints at bad judgment, inadequate management skills, dishonesty, or other character flaws.

Your credit report includes your full name and any other names you've been known by, social security number, current address and previous addresses, current and previous employers, and date of birth. Any criminal history, property ownership and its value, and any professional licenses are also included in some reports.

When a company checks your credit background, they have access to information about your accounts and bill-paying habits with banks, credit card companies, utilities companies, school loans, and mortgages. They will know whether you have ever filed for bankruptcy.

It also lists the names of everyone who has obtained a copy of your report within the past six months to a year. If you authorize more than one potential employer to access your credit report, they may become aware of other companies you've interviewed with.

It is against the law to discriminate against those who have filed bankruptcy, but it is legal to make hiring decisions based on credit history. It is a good guess that in industries where ethics and security play an important role, a bad credit rating will keep you from getting hired. Even the U.S. government uses credit checks to make hiring decisions. The military may discharge or discipline personnel with poor credit reports.

Under the Federal Fair Credit Reporting Act, if information from a Credit Reporting Agency is used against you to deny employment, the person using that information for their decision must tell you they used that information against a favorable decision, and must also tell you which CRA provided the information. This enables you to dispute any erroneous information contained in the report.

CARING FOR A SICK LOVED ONE

At some point in your life, you may have the responsibility of taking care of a sick or elderly loved one. Myra Downs, a healthcare manager for twenty-five years, suggests important steps for caring for your ill loved one while managing your own career.

- **Know your rights.** Understand your employer's family leave policy and know what benefits are available to you before you have to use them.

- **Establish communication.** Anticipate that while dealing with a family illness unexpected events will occur, which might take you away from your job. Keep your boss informed and have a backup plan to accommodate your workload.

- **Inventory your resources.** If you have siblings or family members or church or synagogue contacts, keep them in the loop. These burdens are less heavy when shared.

- **Seek assistance.** Call a hospice in your community and get their advice, which is usually free. There are also many helpful groups such as the Lung Association, Cancer Society, Heart Association, and Alzheimer's Association that can be very supportive and informative. Visit their websites and local offices to educate yourself on what to expect.

- **Keep written schedules for care.** This is especially important if medications are involved. Organization and documentation are critical and will keep everyone clear regarding what has been done and what needs to be done.

IT WORKS FOR ME •

Stay on the sober track

Nancy Waite-O'Brien, Ph.D., director of education and training at the Betty Ford Center, says job-seekers who have a gap in employment due to treatment for substance abuse should be very cautious about telling an employer. Say, "I took some time off to take care of myself," and if pressed further add, "I was under a doctor's care at the time, but the problem has now been taken care of," Waite-O'Brien says.

Once you have returned to the work force, "Don't overexert and take good care of yourself. Practice the HALT strategy and avoid becoming: **H**ungry, **A**ngry, **L**onely, **T**ired."

FINDING A JOB WHEN YOU HAVE A PHYSICAL OR MENTAL ILLNESS

Whether you have a physical or mental illness, or it is a thing of the past, the incident will probably arise when you are faced with explaining the situation to a prospective employer. Though the law is on your side when it comes to discrimination, it may still be an uncomfortable issue during a job search. As unfair as it is, some employers may have prejudices and stereotyped impressions about people with mental or physical illnesses. It is wise to think seriously before you reveal this information.

Remember that any information you give an employer will come from you. You must decide whether or not you need to bring up your illness. The first step is self-assessment. You must determine if you are physically and mentally capable of performing the kinds of jobs you are seeking. You must be aware of your own limitations and seek employment accordingly. If you cannot complete such a self-assessment on your own, seek the help of your healthcare provider.

- Make a list of your physical and emotional limitations. What kind of accommodations do you need? Are you able to handle stress? Spontaneity? Physical labor? Long hours? Can you travel? How long can you concentrate?

- Get feedback from your family and friends on their perspective of what you are capable of regarding your illness. It never hurts to get a second opinion.

- Make a list of possible jobs you could handle based on your physical and emotional limitations. Be aware of assignments or requests you cannot handle.

- Consider your experience, and choose a few of the job possibilities you listed. Request an informational interview with a professional in that position. Ask specific questions such as, "Do you interact with angry and upset customers regularly?" rather than, "How much stress is involved with this position?" Ask about the "next step" in the career path. Just because you could handle this level of employment does not mean you could realistically advance in the career path.

Deciding Whether You Need to Mention It

Once you have completed your personal assessment, you must make the important decision whether or not you need to disclose your illness. If it will in no way affect your performance or ability to do the job, you may decide you do not need to disclose the information. If you think it might, or if you may need assistance from time to time, it is imperative that you let your employer know. If you hide this information and it comes up after you are employed, it could be grounds for dismissal.

- Do not mention an illness in a cover letter, résumé, letter of recommendation, or in a portfolio. These are simply tools to get an employer interested in you.

- Inform your references on whether you want them to mention your illness, and what they should and should not say if it is okay for them to mention it. It is usually the best idea to ask them not to discuss it, or to refer the discussion to you if it comes up.

- It is common to have gaps on your résumé due to time off for an illness. Cover these as truthfully as you can. You can include any volunteer experience, community service, freelance projects, or other experiences you were involved in at that time. If you were raising children at the time, write down "Childcare" to explain the gap. If you simply have nothing to put down, the best option is to leave the gap rather than put down something untruthful or vague. Be prepared as to how you will explain the gap should you be asked.

- Ask your pharmacist if any prescriptions you're taking will register positive on a drug test. Be prepared to share the information beforehand with the lab conducting the test, so they can inform the employer of your disclosure.

Keeping Your Illness Private

It actually takes more preparation if you do not want to disclose your illness. In addition to having explanations for any gaps in work history, you should prepare answers for the questions you most dread. Even think of answers to illegal or direct questions. Do not simply say, "I'd rather not discuss it." The interviewer will think you are hiding something. And you are. You do not want to seem "suspicious." Instead, answer quickly and explain what you learned: "While unemployed for two years, I used the time for personal growth. I developed my interpersonal skills, strengthened my family ties, and continued my education through independent study. I am now ready to reenter the workforce and can bring a strong sense of self, responsibility, and skills to your office."

Imagine the worst-case scenario and prepare for it. Buy a book of interview questions and practice your answers with someone you trust who can coach you.

You should wait until after you are offered the position to bring up your illness or any accommodation you might need. Under the Americans with Disabilities Act (ADA), larger employers are required to meet your request for "reasonable accommodation." This includes altered working hours (allowing you to come in early or stay late to get the workload finished), a workspace without visual or audio distractions (which may consist of a screen or enclosure), break allowances for you to take medications, or more frequent feedback, among others. If you have been offered the position, it is illegal for them not to meet reasonable accommodations.

CHALLENGES FOR OLDER EMPLOYEES

Many employees, age fifty or older, approach the job search with a defeated attitude and a bundle of resentment because of age discrimination. While age discrimination certainly is not fair, a pessimistic or cynical attitude will not help. Don't build your own barriers to success. Here are some common misconceptions that keep older workers from approaching a job search with the positive attitude they need to succeed:

- **Older workers are unwelcome in the workplace.** The facts: Focus on what you have to offer. If *you* focus on your age and consider it a barrier, your interviewers certainly will, too.

- **To get a job, you have to look younger.** The facts: Just be yourself. If you try to dress or act a younger age, you may come across looking awkward and contrived.

- **I know more than my younger boss.** The facts: A condescending attitude will be a turnoff to employers. Yes, as an older worker you have a great deal of experience and insight to offer, but instead of taking on an "I know it all" attitude, show that you are flexible and willing to learn new ideas. You want age to be irrelevant when it comes to being hired, so make age irrelevant when it comes to respecting the boss.

Older workers face many obstacles when it comes to finding a new position. Different employers will have different hang-ups when it comes to hiring an older worker, so know how to circumvent the most common. It's essential to make age irrelevant in the interview process, and there's a lot you can do to achieve this goal.

- **Delete any dates on your résumé that reveal your age.** Make a point to display your knowledge of current industry ideas and skills. Show a high level of enthusiasm and energy, and focus on what you can bring to the position.

- **Market yourself correctly.** Listing all your qualifications and experience can seem intimidating, so only share the most relevant ones. Explain why you think it will be a challenging and fulfilling position. Use your vast experience as rationale for how you'll hit the ground running and inspire others.

- **Don't accept a position that doesn't pay you what you're worth.** Like gender or race, age should never be a determining factor when it comes to salary.

- **Show how the position will help you begin the next phase in your career.** Explain how you would like to develop professionally and how that relates to the position. Discuss your long-term goals.

 **IT WORKS FOR ME** ···

A reason for every year

Bryan Andrews hired a woman in her fifties, older than most of the other applicants, because she arrived at the interview with fifty reasons why she deserved the job. Andrews was impressed by her initiative in self-promotion and the gutsiness of using her age as a sign of extensive experience that would be valuable to the company. The woman had so many strong assets to her credit and was so proud to share them, he says he couldn't pass her up.

BURNOUT

At some point in your career, burnout may sneak up on you. One day it will hit you that you are no longer happy in your job and you will need to decide what to do next. The exhausting what-is-it-all-for-anyway? feeling happens to many career women and can also be a symptom of a midlife crisis. These include:

- Feeling tired all the time

- Unusually cranky and snippy with co-workers

- Abnormal sleep habits, nightmares, and other disturbances

- Difficulty concentrating

- Frequent crying and depression

- Panic attacks

- Feeling of worthlessness

- Weight gain or loss

- Diminished work ethic and productivity

- Decreased sex drive

- Teeth grinding, hair pulling, muscle tension, etc.

- Increased use of drugs or alcohol

- Increased intake of pain relievers and caffeine

- Frequent illness

If you are suffering burnout:

- Go on vacation.

- Decrease your overtime and work hours.

- Communicate with your employer and take on more "fun" responsibilities.

- Boost your own morale by bringing in treats, plants, pictures, and other fun ideas to work with you.

- Relax more outside of the office with bubble baths, movies, or reading.

- Improve your relationships and patch up any hard feelings with co-workers and managers.

- Take a class to improve your work skills and regain enthusiasm for your field.

If your burnout is serious, it may be time for a major life change. Consider switching jobs, career paths, or moving to a new city. Do not make any quick decisions you may regret. Refer back to chapter 3 for advice on changing direction and reinventing your career. Think about what needs to change in your life, and make a plan to accomplish your goal. Think about how much time it will take, how much money, and all the little details to make the change a success.

SO YOU WERE FIRED

You blew it. You made a serious mistake at work and were fired because of it. Maybe you just couldn't perform well enough, maybe you were late every day; maybe it was more serious and you did something illegal. As you know, you certainly are not the first person in history to be fired. You *can* get back on your feet. It's time for some damage control.

- **Wallow in self-pity for a few days.** It's okay to do this . . . for a short time. Then get up, dust yourself off, and get moving.

- **Be honest with yourself.** It does you no good to kid yourself into thinking you were innocent. You were fired for a reason. To move on with your career, you must figure out exactly what that reason was so you can correct the problem. Was it a one-time thing, or do you have a history of a certain negative behavior?

- **Try to patch things up with your last employer.** It is possible that your employer jumped the gun. Maybe she has cooled down enough now to consider giving you your job back under some serious, specific conditions. It never hurts to ask. If you badly burned the bridge with an ugly scene, you should communicate through email, a letter, or a phone message left after work hours. Even if you don't get your job back, it pays to smooth things over, especially if you expect to stay in the same industry.

- **Take the initiative to fix the problem.** Fired for alcohol abuse? Begin rehab or find a 12-step program. Fired for showing up late every day? Take a course on time management. When you go in for future interviews, it will look much better if you have at least sought help for your problem and taken responsibility for your actions.

- **If you were fired for doing something illegal, seek the advice of an attorney.** Depending on the circumstances and the offense, it is possible to get an out-of-court settlement or conditional discharge.

- **Be straight with future employers.** More than likely you will be asked in interviews why you left your previous position. Don't lie. It's possible to verify this information. State in the most positive spin you can give it the reason you were fired. If you continuously missed work, consider saying, "I was terminated because it was challenging to manage my time effectively. I didn't have a good work/life balance and failed at juggling all of my responsibilities. Since then, I've taken time management courses and I've experienced a dramatic improvement with terrific satisfaction in this area."

• **Get creative.** If you have been fired repeatedly, or committed a serious act, you will have to take a few steps back and try again. Ask friends, family, and networking contacts if you could work for them for a probationary period at low pay. Consider freelancing. Take what you can get and slowly rebuild your trustworthiness the old-fashioned way.

• **Look for help.** If you are seeking work after jail time, get help from probation officers and other counseling services.

Laid Off

Today, the stigma of being laid off has diminished. It is quite common for companies to downsize and it doesn't necessarily reflect the actions of the employee. Do not feel this is something you need to hide or feel ashamed of.

• **Wish your co-workers good luck.** Leave on an optimistic and positive note. Do not act as though you are being fired. You want to secure as many contacts and future references as possible.

• **Get on the phone.** Send out a mass email and inform friends and business contacts why you were laid off before they receive misinformation from another source. Let everyone know how they can reach you in the future and what kinds of positions you hope to pursue.

• **Do not encourage people to feel sorry for you.** Pity will not earn you the respect you need to get a job.

• **Take people up on their offers.** Especially in the beginning, people will offer to take you to lunch and send news your way. This is a golden networking opportunity that you should take advantage of while it lasts.

- **Wait for the one you want.** Avoid the temptation to take any job offer that comes your way out of fear of not having a job.

- **Plan something positive to keep your spirits up.** The weekend after your last day, go on a trip or a shopping spree. If you're watching your budget, spend the day relaxing in a museum. This will refresh your energy.

- **Establish a daily routine until you have your next position.** Include "work hours" when you will search for jobs and assign yourself tasks. Set realistic goals such as when you will have your résumé complete, how many letters you will send out each day, and when you hope to have your first interview.

PITFALLS TO PONDER

Keeping it quiet

"My first layoff was brutal. I kept thinking, 'This can't happen to me. I worked hard and I never had any disciplinary issues.' I was handed a white envelope with my final paycheck—not a penny of severance. I left my former office building with my entire desk, and confidence level, reduced to the size of a cardboard box.

"I only told my best friend of the day's ordeal. I decided I'd shoulder the burden and stress without involving anyone else, especially my mom. Not that she would've cast judgment, but it would have stressed her out immensely and she was in no financial position to help. Speaking of finances, I had zero in savings—zip, zilch.

"It was so hard 'living the lie'—pretending to friends and family that I was still working. I felt like a loser being in public places during work hours. I felt as if people were thinking, 'She must have been laid off or else she wouldn't be grocery shopping right now.'

"Then it dawned on me: Keeping my layoff a secret was actually hurting me more than I imagined. If no one knew of my situation, how could they help me? It was hard getting over the negative stigma I had associated with layoffs but surprisingly enough, the more people I told the easier it became. I eventually landed a job and despite experiencing two more layoffs, still had enough confidence in my abilities. I'm now in control of my destiny." —Gina LaPlante, a training and development professional in Atlanta

Telling friends and loved ones about your layoff is the first step in dealing with your own feelings as well as an essential component to finding a new job. Your tone and demeanor will reveal even more than the words you choose. Be calm and measured. Take comfort in knowing that you're not alone. This is most likely not a reflection of you personally or your performance, but more an unfortunate sign of the times.

Talking to your partner. This should be the first person to hear your news. Finances are likely to be a primary concern since that often determines to what degree a family might panic. Be sure you know the details of your severance or unemployment payout to hopefully allay any worry, at least short term. Beyond the money, a partner may pressure you to job-search round-the-clock. He or she might question how you're using your time or balk at what appears to be minimal time spent networking or even interviewing. A stay-at-home partner could resent an invasion of his or her space. On the flip side, you might be expected to contribute much more to household chores or errands to which you're not accustomed. To avoid adding strain to an already stressful situation, talk openly about these or other anticipated problems. Work out a schedule that accommodates both of you with realistic expectations.

Talking to children. When Mom or Dad is out of work and angry, kids of all ages know it. Instead of leaving them to wonder about what it all means, you must be proactive in offering information and assurances about their short- and long-term future. One of the top fears is moving away from school and friends. Encourage your children to ask questions, and answer them as honestly as possible without burdening them with too many unnecessary details. Try to maintain a fairly normal routine to avoid inconveniences or ups and downs in their traditional schedule. Carve out workspace to devote to your job search and set boundaries on your availability. Just because Mom is out of work doesn't mean you're available 24/7 to drive carpool, hit the mall, or toss a ball. Your work is focused on finding a job, which means you can't always jump on a moment's notice.

Talking to friends. Friends often don't know what to say and are afraid of adding insult to injury. Sometimes that means they'll avoid calling or making the first move. Knowing this in advance, you should take the initiative to let them know your status and even ask for their help. One option for breaking the ice: "Perhaps you've heard the news. My company just went through a layoff and unfortunately I'm one of the unlucky ones." Don't dwell on the negative details.

Keep a positive tone and attitude—now is not the time to trash your former employer's management style—since you'll soon be asking for friends to assist in your search. They're much more likely to extend a helping hand to an upbeat pal than an angry, bitter one.

STILL CAN'T GET A JOB?

Don't let a long job search discourage you. It's easy to become frustrated and lose hope when you've been searching for months, even a year. Though it can be scary and frustrating, try not to develop a pessimistic attitude. Employers will sense your negativity and be less likely to hire you. Staying positive and focused is the single must important aspect of surviving a lengthy job search. If you feel defeated, you will be defeated.

Take into consideration that the average job search can last up to six months, even longer in a bad economy. Many people think that they will have a job within a month and do not prepare themselves emotionally or financially for such a long stretch of unemployment.

Make sure your job search is not halfhearted. Set goals for yourself and stick with it. Looking for a job should be your full-time job. You should be spending at least twenty to thirty hours a week on your job search, sending out résumés, networking, and going on interviews. Maybe it is time to pick up the pace. Persistence pays off when it comes to job hunting. If you are sending out résumés and job searching diligently and getting no bites, you may need to switch tactics. Get your résumé critiqued. Make sure you are applying for jobs you are qualified for. Network more.

One possibility: You may be dedicating too much time applying for advertised jobs. Only about 20 percent of jobs are advertised, so only 20 percent of your job-searching time should be spent responding to classified ads and Internet-posted positions. The rest of your time should be spent networking and looking for jobs that aren't advertised.

 IT WORKS FOR ME ···

Don't give up

"When a door shuts, a window usually opens. Even when you don't get the job, stay in touch with those contacts. I interviewed with a company where the people and the job description were an ideal match. The interviews went very well, but they didn't offer me the position because I lacked just one more year of experience than was required. Because I had established good chemistry with the company, we began talking about project-based work, and they hired me in a contract position." —Courtney Perry, account supervisor, Ketchum

If the bills are starting to overwhelm you and your attitude has fallen through the floor, it may be time to get a part-time job. You may not have worked as a waitress, delivery person, retail sales clerk, or grocery stocker since you were in school, so the idea is probably not appealing. You are not giving up, or settling. Keep looking for a "real" job while you work part-time.

- **A part-time job can provide much-needed income.** Though they don't all pay well, some income is certainly more than no income.

- **A part-time job will get you out of the house.** Remember that not all rewards to having a job are financial. It may improve your happiness and self-esteem enough to land the job you were hoping for.

● **You will meet new contacts.** Many part-time jobs, such as retail sales or consulting, can lead to full-time positions. For example, you may start at the Gap as a sales clerk and work your way up through the ranks, ultimately to a human resources manager, the exact position you were hoping for.

● **A part-time job will prevent a lengthy gap on your résumé.** Even if it doesn't add skills for your career path, potential employers will respect your work ethic and ability to adapt.

IT WORKS FOR ME

Overcoming obstacles

"The start of 2002 was a definite obstacle. My husband left me, my father passed, and I had been unemployed for almost nine months. Motivated and determined to push forward for the sake of my one-year-old son, I continued my job search, and despite what I felt about temp agencies, I had applied to many. I had just about given up after enduring many tests and interviews until I got a phone call from an agency. I've been working with them for several months doing long-term assignments, and am pretty confident about getting something permanently. My son and I are happier. I'm able to provide for him, and we love our new place. I see the past year as not only an obstacle but as a test of strength."
—Kalimba Pegues, newly satisfied professional

Prevention Is the Best Cure

Good decision-making from the onset often helps to prevent mistakes and curveballs from occurring. That said, if we were all blessed with 20/20 hindsight we wouldn't make erroneous decisions to begin with. With that in mind, here are some thoughts on making savvy moves and, when necessary, preventing your existing troubles from wreaking more havoc in your life.

MAKE GOOD DECISIONS

Some curveballs could have been avoided had we simply made the right decisions in the first place. We've all heard the adage "Prevention is the best cure." Even if the curveball couldn't have been avoided, great decision-making abilities will certainly help you solve your problems (not to mention improve your work performance).

- **Be aware that you need to make a decision.** Don't just let things fall into place. Often decisions seem gradual, but at some point you have to decide if you should continue on the course in front of you, or change paths. Example: Your teenager is getting into more and more trouble at school and in the community. Realize this means you need to make a decision, not simply pray that the issue goes away.

- **Think about the importance of the decision.** Why is it an important decision? What will happen if you don't "make it" but let the situation take its own course? Who will be affected in this decision? What can you gain or lose? Example: If you do nothing, your child might not graduate and could get into serious legal trouble.

- **Make a list of all possible choices.** Be flexible and creative and don't try to rule anything out just yet. Even if you initially don't think it is a great choice, write it down. Example: You could hire a tutor, change schools, or seek counseling.

- **Think of where you could research possibilities.** Arm yourself with information. Turn to friends and family, co-workers, counselors, agencies, books, articles, and other research materials. Learn from the experience of others. Revise your list of possible choices to add or cross out options based on what you learn. Example: After speaking with teachers, guidance counselors, and family members, you realize a peer counselor isn't an effective solution for your son.

- **Weigh the pros and cons of all your alternatives.** Keep in mind your values and priorities. Put them in order from best to worst alternatives. Picture the outcome of each choice. Example: If you get a tutor, your teenager's grades may improve but will it help your child choose better friends?

• **Think about how realistic each choice is.** What would you have to do to enact each alternative? Cross out any unrealistic choices. Example: Can you afford private school?

• **Find a choice that suits you the most.** Weigh the outcome against what each choice entails. Is the outcome worth the effort? Example: Can you leave work early on Fridays to supervise who your teenager is spending time with after school?

• **Enact it.** Once you have made a decision, the sooner you get started the better. Break it into little pieces and start with step one.

• **Take time to think about how the decision is going.** Is it everything you thought it would be or do you need to try something else?

Here are some mistakes to avoid when making important decisions:

• **Don't rely too much on experts.** They may not know what's best for you and may not know your situation well enough. "Expert" information can easily be taken out of context.

• **Don't put too much value on anyone's opinion.** Mother does not know everything. Not everyone who gives you information has the same beliefs and priorities as you do.

• **Don't underestimate someone's opinion.** You may have a preconceived notion about someone that leads you to disregard what he thinks. He may not be the smartest person you've ever met, but it may still be great advice.

• **Don't be limited to your expectations.** Don't let personal biases or preconceived notions limit your ability to think things through. Weigh all information objectively. Be open to hearing information you don't necessarily want to think about.

- **Don't ignore your intuition.** You may have picked up on something in your subconscious that hasn't reached your conscious thought process. The human brain is a sponge that absorbs more information than our conscious thought can register. Sometimes gut feelings are formed on this information, so it is wise to pay attention to intuition.

Your best bet is to face curveballs by seeking advice specific to your situation. There are exceptional professionals to help you overcome any number of personal challenges, before they destroy your career.

- **If you find yourself in financial trouble, seek help.** Ask trusted friends and family members to recommend a savvy financial planner. Make an appointment to discuss your situation and seek their advice on options for the future. Your bank might also offer such services. It's always good to get more than one opinion. A lawyer might also be able to help with debt-related concerns.
- **Substance abuse.** There is an extensive resource section on the Betty Ford Center's website, which can be found at bettyfordcenter. org. It is frequently updated and includes articles and organizations to assist with all types of addiction.

CHAPTER TEN

Put Your Mouth Where the Money Is
Speak Up to Get What You Deserve

"When you undervalue what you do, the world will undervalue who you are."
— SUZE ORMAN,
financial guru

According to the 2002 U.S. Census Bureau, women earned 76 cents for every $1 men in the same position earned, in full-time year-round positions in 2001. Even though this broke the record as an all-time high, we say women are still not getting their due when it comes to money. One possible reason women are paid less for the same positions and represent only 12 percent of management jobs—even though we comprise almost 50 percent of the workforce—is that women tend to be less effective at negotiation.

Studies show that women are just as good at negotiating as men—except when it comes to negotiating for ourselves. We're outspoken when it comes to haggling for a great deal at a flea market or speaking up to raise money for our kids' schools. Yet, when the focus is on us, we become shy, intimidated, and uncomfortable. Among the most common challenges: downplaying our worth, failing to research comparable compensation, aiming to please others at our own expense, and settling for what others think we deserve instead of for what we want. We'll address various tactics for understanding and overcoming these serious issues with the goal of empowering women to be their own best negotiators. We'll cover asking for and responding to raises and effectively handling bonuses and performance reviews. Since women often ignore a host of benefits available to them simply because they don't understand or value them, we'll explain how to identify, evaluate, and negotiate perks beyond money.

Negotiation Is the Missing Link

MISTAKES WOMEN MAKE

Cynthia Stevens, an associate professor at the Robert H. Smith School of Business at the University of Maryland, says in a negotiation, women tend to be more indirect when asking for things than men. "For example, a man might say, 'I want more money,' whereas women might say, 'I really have a lot of expenses because of the move.' Women will infer what they want, but not come out and ask for it. Women are also more likely to take 'no' for an answer. They hear no and stop. Men might try to offer a different counteroffer."

Stevens believes that women set lower goals and are satisfied with less, but it's not clear why. "One theory is that women compare themselves to other women and they don't include men when comparing salaries, benefits, or promotions. For some reason, women tend to think lower pay is fair."

Stevens says that men can be easily taught to set higher goals simply by saying, "You need to set higher goals." But women, she says, want to be taught the steps and tools to set a *fair* goal. Women need to learn to reach higher goals.

One scenario Stevens often poses in her negotiation courses: I am constrained geographically because my spouse just got a job here. My job must be in this city.

"Women interpret this scenario with a willingness to accept a low salary and benefits or even a job they don't want as long as it meets the basic criteria of being in that city. Men, on the other hand, say they'd stand firm and wait for a job to come along in that city that meets their higher requirements and goals."

Most of the mistakes women make in negotiation happen before they even enter the conversation. Stevens says women don't set a "BATNA," which is the Best Alternative to a Negotiated Agreement. A BATNA is any alternative choice to taking the position. If you go into a negotiation without a good BATNA, it is all or nothing. You will have convinced yourself that you have nothing to fall back on and therefore you must accept whatever they offer. Acting this way "instills fear and takes away your 'choice.' This will be reflected in the negotiation by your attitude and they will know they 'have you.'" Stevens's advice for creating your own BATNA:

- Try to generate another job offer.

- Line up another interview.

- Take an "I'm the buyer" approach to the negotiation.

- Be aware of how eager you sound and act from the very first contact, letters, résumé, and phone calls all the way through the interviews and negotiations.

- Think of the type of setting you're most comfortable in and try to have important conversations there. What environment is it easiest for you to stand firm or say no in?

It's also essential to prepare specific things to say depending on the style of your negotiator. You should have a plan of attack for both. "A hard-style negotiator is firmer and gruffer with forbidding body language and tends to say no to everything," says Stevens. "This type of person can be very intimidating to women." A soft-style is "very agreeable and tries to work with you."

But, cautions Stevens, don't be fooled by this pleasant personality. "It's a common mistake with women who have soft-style negotiators to be very agreeable in return, trying to be polite, match them and make them like you. You can easily end up walking away with less. The bottom line is you still have to ask for what you want without feeling guilty regardless of who you're dealing with."

Most of the mistakes women make when it comes to negotiating have little to do with their negotiating skills, but with their negotiation attitudes. Review the following list of mistakes women make and compare them with your own feelings and attitudes toward negotiation. You cannot correct your own mistakes unless you can recognize them.

- **Women tend not to recognize opportunities to negotiate.** Do not make the mistake of considering all salary and benefit offers as firm. It is not a take-it-or-leave-it situation. Most employers expect you to come back with a counteroffer.

- **Women are good at building relationships.** When women value a relationship, they tend to protect it. Women make the mistake of failing to negotiate out of fear of hurting the relationship they have built with their interviewer and potential employer. Do not make the mistake of thinking negotiation will anger your interviewer.

- **Society has taught women to shy away from bold behavior.** Women are more likely to sit back and wait for credit for their work, than to ask for compensation. Women have internalized the idea that asking for more than what someone wants to give is rude. Realize that it is okay to ask for what you deserve.

- **Women fail to do their homework.** An important part of salary and negotiation is researching comparable salaries in similar positions. Many women do not know their own worth. Make sure you value your own experiences and education.

- **Women focus less on what they are giving the employer than on what the employer is giving them.** They already see the employer as providing so much that they are willing to settle for smaller salaries. Focus on what you are offering an employer, not how the position will advance your career.

- **Women start off in the hole.** Women do not negotiate a higher salary to begin with, so raises and bonuses computed by percentage are smaller as well. The problem feeds off itself and the wage gap between men and women continues to grow larger. Don't make the mistake of thinking a low salary will eventually "catch up" to what you deserve.

• **Women take negotiations personally.** Remember it is about business, not your own personal worth. Detach your emotions from the conversation.

PITFALLS TO PONDER

Failing to negotiate can cost you the job

"In many positions, especially at manager level and above, you lose credibility with potential employers if you don't negotiate. This is a skill many people will need to perform their duties, and it's really a great test of how you will negotiate on behalf of your company if you are hired. Companies expect you to negotiate and you must have enough confidence in your abilities and contributions to at least try. The worst they can say is 'no.'" —Caroline Brown, manager, employment marketing, The Home Depot

More than likely, you make at least a few of these mistakes. Chances are, interviewers have more experience and skill at salary negotiation than you will. It is important to prepare a strategy.

Negotiating is not a simple process. It takes a lot of research, effort, great debating skills and practice, but the payoff is worth the work. Never accept a job offer without discussing the salary and benefits. Go in prepared.

CONDUCT RESEARCH

The negotiation process revolves around two factors: what you are worth and what they are willing to pay for you. To negotiate successfully, take these factors into consideration and research them thoroughly. It is one of the few steps in the negotiation process that you have full control over. Would you take a test without studying?

The first step in researching these two factors is to consider the position. Know the required skills and job responsibilities, and the company's goals, clients, mission statement, and any other details you can find. Use this information as perspective or context for your research. You may have handled layout and design of the newsletter at your previous position—a very impressive responsibility, but only if it is relevant to the position you are applying for. If it's not, you shouldn't expect to be compensated for it.

What Are You Worth?

- **Make a list of your credentials.** What degrees do you have? What other training or education do you have? If you held an impressive title in the past, use it to your advantage. Did you have a respected position with your previous employer? Did you work for a well-known, successful company?

- **What measurable successes have you had in your previous positions?** Did you raise sales by 15 percent? Did you save your company $50,000? Did you organize a seminar for one thousand guests? The eye is drawn to numbers and statistics, so include as many as you can.

- **What is included in your skills set?** Make sure you can meet every responsibility of the job and can provide specific examples of the skills you have to fulfill them.

- **Think value-added.** Maybe you can bring excellent finance experience with you to a human resources position. Do you have any technology specialties or marketing know-how? Are you bilingual? If so, you may deserve higher compensation.

- **What is your work ethic like?** Are you willing to come in early, stay late? Can you be counted on in a crisis? If you can document this or provide references, it may increase your worth.

Knowing what you are worth is crucial in knowing what you deserve. Do not underestimate what you can offer to a company. Writing out your skills and experience on paper can help you objectively evaluate how much you should be earning. Your salary range should match what you're worth.

When you are in the interview, briefly and clearly list the most impressive qualifications you have as supporting material for the salary you are requesting. Show them exactly why you deserve the salary you are asking for. Show them what a bargain you are.

How Much Are They Willing to Pay?

Sometimes you will know the salary before you go in for the interview. Don't simply accept this at face value. You can still negotiate. Think of it as a ballpark figure. If it is lower than you had hoped for, don't walk away from the position. Go in prepared to negotiate based on what you can bring to the position.

If you do not know the salary going into the interview, you need to research salaries in similar companies and positions. More than likely, the company you are interviewing with will have done similar research. Take into consideration geographic location and cost-of-living, degree level, years of experience required, and size of company. All these factors will influence salary averages. If you live in Smalltown, USA, do not expect to be paid the same amount of money for the same position with the same responsibilities as someone in Bigtown, USA.

There are many sources to research salaries. Some are free, others available only to paying customers. Your local library should have references. Online resources include:

- *wetfeet.com*

- *salary.com*

- *rileyguide.com*

- *careers.wsj.com*

- *bls.gov/oco/*

It is not enough simply to research comparable salaries. You need to bring this information to the interview. Be prepared for your interviewer to argue the validity of your research because of factors dissimilar to the position you are applying for. Like all statistics, salary research has room for error. Do not use comparable salaries as the sole basis of your salary requirement. It must be combined with information about your skills and the responsibilities of the job.

Use this information to predetermine a salary range. Know the lowest offer you are willing to accept, the offer you think you deserve, and the offer you will be thrilled with. Prepare materials, charts, data, etc., to bring with you as support for your salary request. It will be easier to persuade people if you can show them solid, objective information.

You are not just there to sell yourself. You are there to get information as well. Here is a list of questions you need to have answered in the negotiation conversation:

- What is included in the salary and benefits package? When do I become eligible for benefits?

- How much vacation time and sick leave will I receive? Can I roll it over or cash it out if I don't use it?

- Is there a 401(k) plan or retirement program? How much can I contribute and what percentage is matched?

- What deductions are taken out of the paycheck and how much does it add up to?

- How often will I be paid?

- When will I receive a review and be eligible for a raise?

- What are the opportunities for advancement?

- Are there bonus opportunities?

- Is there a credit union I can join?

The Dreaded Question

It is probable that you will be asked your salary history at some point. If you were underpaid in your previous position, you may not want to reveal this information. Employers may base their offer on what you were previously making, or on the flip side, assume they can't afford you. You want the employer to base their offer on your value, not your previous salary.

- Let the interviewer ask *you* about salary. Be prepared to answer the question.

- Do not lie about your salary history. They can verify this information.

- If you do not wish to tell your salary history, answer with the salary range you are willing to negotiate within. If it is a reasonable range, they will more than likely drop the question of salary history.

- Do not become defensive or refuse to answer the question. It will leave a bad impression and only make the interviewer more interested in your salary history.

- Talk about how your salary increased over time, how you received off-cycle adjustments, or bonuses.

BROACHING THE SUBJECT OF SALARY

Some companies will ask for salary requirements in a cover letter. Some will actually ask you to accept the offer before they even mention the word *salary*. There is no routine, no schedule for when companies will discuss salary with you. There is, however, an ideal.

It is to your best advantage to hold off on discussing salary until after you have been offered the position. Wait for them to bring it up, and try not to be the first to mention a range. Of course, the process rarely works this way. It is a little messier, a little more random, so you need to be prepared with information on how to handle every situation.

If you are asked to name your salary requirement in a cover letter or résumé, do so. It may be the criteria used to weed out résumés. If you do not include the information at all, your résumé will be quickly set aside. Put down a reasonable range such as $55,000 to $65,000, depending upon the responsibilities of the position.

If your interviewer brings up salary before you are prepared to discuss it, try to sidestep the question. Say something along the lines of, "Actually, I'd like to know more about the position before I can give you that answer." Then ask a question about the job's responsibilities.

Once you have been offered the position, and it is time to discuss the salary, you want them to name a figure first. This prevents you from naming a sum lower than they had been willing to pay, or a sum that is too high.

- Ask what the typical range is for others in the company with that position.

- Ask what they had budgeted for that job.

- Say you will consider any reasonable offer.

- Say that they are better informed to determine how much you are worth to the company than yourself.

All of these statements turn the situation around politely. It puts them in the position of naming a range first. If they counter, simply move on to the next statement. More than likely, they will return the question back to you no more than three times before they state a salary range.

You Named a Figure Too Early
You messed up and named a figure too early. After some research, you found out that you deserve more, and they were probably expecting to pay more. The time has come for the negotiation. Now what? How do you go back and ask for more when you have already named a figure?

- Try to ignore the earlier figure. Don't mention it if they don't.

- Explain that you didn't realize the full responsibilities of the job. Now that you have more information on the level of the position and what it entails, that sum is no longer relevant. Then state the salary you think you deserve.

- Explain that you have done more market research, cost-of-living research, and researched salaries in similar positions, and have readjusted the salary figure accordingly.

Remember that it was your mistake. You did say you would accept that salary, so you need to be willing to compromise. Rather than refusing the offer, ask if you could have a review and salary increase after three months rather than six. Ask if you can have a higher percentage raise increase the first year to make up the difference. You should decide beforehand whether you are willing to accept the sum you stated before you did your research, or whether you want to walk away and apply your newfound knowledge the next time.

PITFALLS TO PONDER

An angry interviewer

"In the interview or negotiation process, pay attention to your body language and to theirs, too. A lot of people will nod their head yes when listening. Don't make this mistake since it implies that you're agreeing with what your interviewer says and makes it more difficult for you to say no or offer a counter later on. You've already said yes unwittingly. Instead of nodding, communicate with words.

"If you make a mistake, back up and correct it. Some mistakes are not retractable. Once you've consciously agreed to something, you can't really go back. Be a person of your word." —Cynthia Stevens, associate professor, Robert H. Smith School of Business, University of Maryland

PITFALLS TO PONDER

Check your emotions

Your attitude and approach in a negotiation set the tone of the conversation. Make sure you approach the situation with the right attitude and never negotiate when you are UNFOCUSED:

Unrealistic

Negative

Frantic

Overly eager

Carefree

Unorganized

Stressed

Excited

Desperate

ALL ABOUT ATTITUDE

When it comes time to negotiate salary, your approach and attitude can make or break the conversation. One of the mistakes women make is to take negotiation personally. This can lead to an aggressive or defensive tone, which will put off your interviewer. The goal is to not let the conversation become an argument.

- **Be persuasive.** Keep the focus on how you can benefit the organization. You want to accentuate what you are giving, not what you are taking. Discuss their needs first and articulate how you can help the bottom line.

- **Stay positive.** Smile. Make good eye contact. You want everyone to leave the interview with a good impression of the exchange. It shows that you are mature and reasonable.

- **Let the conversation flow naturally.** You don't want your answers to sound contrived or rehearsed.

- **Remain calm no matter what is said.** If you do not act cool under pressure, your interviewer may take it as a sign of how you handle stress and deadlines in the future.

- **Show enthusiasm and excitement.** Let the employer think the only thing keeping you from taking the job is the salary and benefits. Show your interest in the position. Employers want to hire someone who is excited about the job.

- **Do not list your expenses or details about your personal life.** Saying that you are recently divorced and need more money to support your children will put a damper on the positive and energetic tone of the interview—and frankly, this information is not relevant to the employer.

Visualize yourself already having the position. This will help curb the feeling that you will lose the position if you try to negotiate the salary you deserve. Think of negotiation as a joint problem you are solving with the employer. You are not competing on different sides. You both want the same thing: for you to take the position at a reasonable salary. This creates the perfect recipe for compromise. The likelihood of the conversation being a success is high. So relax.

IT WORKS FOR ME

Identify a negotiation coach

"The confidence you need comes by doing your research and being able to articulate the concrete, measurable value your skills bring to the table. I've found it's helpful to find someone who takes pride in their negotiating skills. For me, early in my career, it was my father, a career salesman, who encouraged me to 'go for it' when it felt so uncomfortable. These people are helpful when it comes time to negotiating your offer. They can give you the confidence to push when you don't really want to and they can provide creative ideas when you feel that you do not have it in you." —Caroline Brown, manager, employment marketing, The Home Depot

GO IN WITH A PLAN

Based on your research and self-evaluation, you should go into negotiations with several salary and benefits options you are willing to consider. Now is the time for the give and take, to set one of those options into action.

- Consider the first offer. Many people automatically reject the first offer on the table for more, but if it is exactly what you were hoping for, you should take it. Don't make things more difficult than they have to be.

- If the first offer is not what you were hoping for, remain silent. The employer may become uncomfortable enough with your silence to up the ante without you even having to say a word.

- Start high. You need to have room to maneuver. The higher you start, the higher salary you are likely to get.

- If they begin with a very low offer, do not be tricked into thinking your ideal is too high. This is their goal. Stick to your research and the salary you decided you were willing to accept. Do not go lower than what you had planned. Understand what your "walk away" number is.

- Remain flexible. Be willing to trade salary for benefits. Keep in mind that you can negotiate the timeline of future raises, promotions, and reviews, or a signing bonus to make up for a lower salary. Keep in mind at all times what is the most important detail to you and know what you are willing to let go.

- Go in with a stash of credentials and research. If they are not accepting your offers, pull out letters of recommendation, remind them of your qualifications, and show them your research. Have justification for your requests.

- Expect a period when it seems you will not get your request. It is quite common to have a "stalemate" for a length of time in the conversation. Don't despair. Hold out for the next step when the compromising begins.

- Just when you think you have reached an agreement, be ready for the employer to start backpedaling on minor concessions made previously. They will try to slip them in. Stand firm. If they ask to go back on something, match the request with a little detail you would like to go back on. It may seem nitpicky, but the little details can really add up.

- Make it easy for them to back down and meet your offers. Make suggestions such as, "If you will pay me X amount in salary, I'd be willing to let go of Y benefits." You want to appear to be fair and reasonable.

- If you are offered a "final" offer, consider it for a few moments, then calmly state again what you would be willing to accept. If they are serious about that being the "final" offer, they will repeat it. If you are not ready to give an answer, ask if you can have time to think about it.

Throughout the entire conversation, sell yourself. Provide specifics why you are the best person for the job. Give examples of what you have achieved in the past and what you plan to accomplish if you accept the position. Tell them what you can add to their organization. Paint a picture of yourself in the job, so they visualize you working for them.

Tell them how great they will be for using you. Not, "I will be an asset to your company," but, "You have so much potential, together we can maximize it to everyone's advantage." Say, "Your investment in me is an investment in our future" instead of, "I want a higher salary and more benefits." Get your point across, make them part of the process, and most importantly, avoid stepping over that invisible line between persuasive and obnoxious.

If you are working with an employment agency, use them to do the negotiating for you. You still need to keep these tactics in mind, but agencies can facilitate communication between you and an employer to everyone's advantage.

IT WORKS FOR ME

Negotiate work/family issues before you've been hired

"It is always more difficult to negotiate out-of-the-ordinary working conditions when you are a new hire," say Deborah M. Kolb, Judith Williams, and Carol Frohlinger, the principals of TheShadowNegotiation.com, which includes books, courses, and workshops to advance women's negotiation skills. "A company has less incentive to meet conditions set by a relatively unknown or untested applicant. But there are several things you can do to improve the situation."

The principals offer two specific tactics to better your chances of getting what you want. The first is to demonstrate the value you bring to the organization. "The incentive to negotiate with you is directly correlated with the perception of your worth to the organization. You may want the job *and* the flexible schedule, but the company has to believe that it would be getting something of equal value in return. It is your job to make that case—to put your value right there on the table where it becomes obvious."

It's equally important to appear flexible. "The more ways you can give the other person to say yes, the better your chances are that he or she will. It helps to understand the kinds of resistance you are likely to encounter and be prepared to offer options that solve those problems. Consider an experiment or trial as one option with guidelines and a timeline for evaluation."

TAKE IT OR LEAVE IT

If you cannot negotiate a mutually acceptable offer with the employer, consider whether you need to walk away. Even if you really need a job, even if you are feeling pressured by your family to accept an offer, do not settle for less than you are worth, less than you would be offered somewhere else. You will just end up searching for a job again in the very near future.

- Rejecting the offer may be the best negotiating tactic there is. They may come back with the offer you were hoping for rather than let you walk away. It is expensive and time-consuming for employers to interview candidates. They would prefer to fill the position as soon as possible.

● Even though you refused the position, send a thank-you note a few days later restating the salary you would be willing to accept and reiterating your interest in the position and the company. After they have thought about it for a few days, your salary requirement may seem more reasonable than they had originally thought.

● Be careful not to burn any bridges. If you stay on good terms, you may get a call a few months down the road for a similar position with a better salary. Conduct yourself professionally at all times.

It May Be a Dream Job, But Is It Your Dream Job?

When we buy a new dress or any other piece of clothing, we go to great lengths to make sure it's the right fit. We inspect ourselves from every imaginable angle in the mirror to confirm a proper complement to all body parts. From the neckline to the hemline, nothing escapes our eye.

Even higher standards must be applied when evaluating a job offer. Instead of arms, elbows, hips, butts, thighs, knees, and toes, you'll want to look beyond cash compensation to seven other categories that relate to the position you're considering. This is a sure way to determine if it's the best possible fit.

● **Functional fit.** Work is much less fun and fulfilling when you're doing stuff you absolutely hate or when you're performing tasks that are uncomfortable to you. Will you be playing to your strengths? Does the thought of doing this type of work make you giddy with glee that someone is actually willing to pay you to do what you love? Does the position offer enough stimulation or challenge? Is the title and level of responsibility in line with what you deserve?

● **Industry.** More and more we see that women care very much about the type of work they do in terms of industry. Perhaps you're an accountant, but you couldn't get excited about doing the books in any old field. Your passion lies within the nonprofit world, and that's where you'd be most effective in fulfilling your functional fit. Similarly, an ace marketing and branding professional might not feel comfortable applying her skills and expertise at a tobacco giant if she's a nonsmoker. Be sure the industry doesn't conflict with your personal beliefs and values.

- **Employer.** Research their position in the marketplace. Are they a leader in their respective industry experiencing terrific growth, or is their stock taking a dive amid mass layoffs? If it's a large player, figure out how the media reports on them. At the other end of the spectrum, if you're talking to a small company, look at their products, services, and clients as a first step in determining the strength of their finances.

- **Management and supervisor(s).** High turnover or great loyalty and longevity among employees is a telltale sign of the respect given to management at any employer. While interviewing with the person who'd serve as your direct boss, what were your immediate thoughts and observations on his or her management and work styles? Did you sense any concern about the potential of conflicts or clashes? Ask to speak to others who have worked for that person. If in doubt, it's essential to address it and work it out up front so both of you are crystal clear on expectations.

PITFALLS TO PONDER

Don't suffer a bully boss

"I find it is not so much the money and traditional benefits that keep me in my job, but the work environment and the quality of life the company offers. If you have ever worked for an overbearing, micromanaging boss, you will know what I mean," says marketing pro Marilyn Muller. "When that happened to me, I addressed the issues with my boss and the company I was working for. I got the cold shoulder even though we had an 'open door' policy. I gave what I considered an appropriate amount of time to address the problems then decided to leave." The moral to Muller's story: "Consider taking a small pay cut or lateral move to improve your situation. I did and it paid off in spades in the long run."

- **Advancement and growth opportunity.** Most of us have a long-term plan, and the ideal position will mesh nicely with our goals. Sometimes a job is ideal because it affords us the opportunity to gain new skills and experience that will be essential toward achieving the ultimate position. Will this employer provide internal or external training and development to complement your existing skill set? If you're just launching a career or are in a mid-career transition, will this position be an effective bridge to the next step? Beyond assessing this particular position, you'll also want to know if the company has a formal policy for promoting from within. This often sheds light on your potential opportunity for growth at this particular employer.

- **Culture.** Dress code, workspace, office hours, and employee diversity all contribute to the culture of any organization. Will you work seventy-hour weeks in a T-shirt and jeans? Are family picnics and an active commitment to the community part of the routine? Is there a sense of teamwork and camaraderie, or is everything and everyone independent and autonomous? Do your best to determine the values of the organization by talking to current and former employees, studying the "About Us" section of its website, and reading media accounts and annual reports.

- **Location.** While this may seem relatively unimportant compared to some of the other criteria, a long commute can make your job miserable. Make the drive (or train, bus, or subway ride) a few times during rush hour, not just in the middle of the day, to get a realistic sense of what you'd be in for. If you're hoping for a telecommuting arrangement, it's important to negotiate this up front—or at the very least, to broach the subject contingent upon a satisfactory orientation and initial completion of mutual goals.

Before you accept a position, consider the size of the company. Whether a small or large company is right for you may depend on your career stage, as well as your personality.

- Large companies often offer great training programs for entry-level positions, affording time for adjustment from the theoretical realm of college to the practical world of work.

- The resources in terms of equipment, facilities, and funds available at a large corporation can be a significant factor in fields such as engineering, IT, or medical research.

- There's more diversity in a big company. For those less comfortable with close personal interactions, there's also more anonymity.

- At a small firm you may feel like you are thrown right into the deep end, where everyone can see if you sink or swim.

- A small office environment requires great responsibility, but provides exposure to a wide variety of tasks. You may learn about all aspects of a business, from soup to nuts, instead of just one piece of the pie.

- Self-starters find there's often less bureaucracy and more autonomy in a small company. Creative types may find it easier to get their ideas off the ground.

 IT WORKS FOR ME

Step right up!

"I got to be vice president at CNN because I built a kingdom when no one was looking. Whenever something came along to be done and no one was doing it, I raised my hand and said, 'I'll see if I can figure it out.' But I didn't step on other people's territory. I went where there was a gap or to places that hadn't been blazed. I did

it because I have a short attention span and I needed new chal-
lenges to keep me going. Once I figured it out, I was then happy to
give it away. A problem most women have is that they hold on to
things forever when it's sometimes better to let go and move on."
—Gail Evans, former executive vice president of the CNN News
Group and best-selling author of *Play Like a Man and Win Like a
Woman: What Men Know About Success That Women Need to
Learn* (Broadway Books, 2001)

- Smaller companies may offer larger salaries or signing bonuses to compensate for the lack of benefits available.

- Some assume that they can achieve a better work/life balance at a small company. While there may be more flexibility in your daily schedule—you can take off an hour to catch the preschool play or go to the dentist's office—there's also no one to cover for you at critical company functions or production times.

- A small office environment can be close-knit (or claustrophobic depending on your personal opinion). Forget standing around gossiping at the water cooler. This office sport is too up-close and personal, and strictly taboo in a small firm. You must be able to get along well with co-workers. At the same time, you may work in closer proximity to company leaders, gaining the benefit of their input and energy.

Once you've decided to accept a position, and have negotiated the salary and benefits you want, get it in writing. The deal is not finalized until it's in writing, so don't give notice at your current position or make any major moves until a contract has been signed.

Benefit from Your Benefits Package

Don't forget to negotiate benefits. Overall, benefits can comprise up to 30 percent of your salary—no small sum. Your compensation should meet all of your needs, not just monetary ones. Consider hiring bonuses, vacation time, retirement plans, sick leave, insurance, and other company benefits as open for negotiation as well. If you are planning to go back to school, tuition reimbursement may be just as important as health insurance. If you're planning to start a family, maternity leave and vacation time may be the most important feature for you. All of these benefits can tip the scale in negotiating salary.

Even if your salary is as much as $10,000 higher than your previous wages, a poor benefits package can deplete much more. For example:

- You may have to pay the monthly health insurance premium for your dependents.

- Consider how much vacation time you'll receive compared to your previous position. An additional week's vacation or other time off can add up to thousands of dollars.

- Consider the average percentage of pay increase you will receive, and the length of the increments between receiving them. You may quickly be earning less than you would have at your previous position.

- If you're offered a signing bonus, there may be higher taxes on it, so you will see a smaller percentage of the money than you might expect. Ask for your signing bonus to be increased to compensate for taxes, so that you receive the full amount and the company covers your tax liability.

KNOW WHAT'S AVAILABLE

To successfully negotiate a benefits package, you have to understand what's out there. Some companies will offer a standard benefits package and others will let you pick and choose the ones you want, "cafeteria style." There is a wide range of benefits from a wide range of companies. Here are some of the most basic:

- Health insurance

- Dental insurance

- Vision plan

- Life insurance

- Retirement plan/401(k) and profit sharing

- Sick leave

- Short- and long-term disability

- Maternity, bereavement, childcare, or eldercare benefits

- Employee assistance programs

- Financial planning services

- Credit union

- Relocation

- Tuition assistance

- Company car

- Paid parking

- Parties, retreats, company packages

- Gym membership or wellness packages

- Free subscriptions, discount offers, tickets, community events

- Severance package

THE BASICS

Most positions will offer insurance, but the package can vary greatly from company to company. Some plans will include dental or vision, others will not. Some will cover the premium for the employee *and* their dependents; others will only cover the employee. Not only does the amount of coverage vary, but the insurance plan will vary as well. Different insurance companies will offer several different plans. Some plans have a deductible, some have a copay, and others don't. The only way to know your plan is to review the documents. *This is critical*. Your human resources department can help you understand the details.

Vacation time and sick leave are also standard in a benefits package. Two weeks' vacation is the norm; the amount of sick leave is more varied. Make sure you are aware of when you start earning the time, how much time you will receive, and when you will receive an increase. Understand how much advance notice you must give to use time off, and if there are certain seasons or periods when you cannot use it. Take into consideration whether or not your unused time off will roll over into the next year or if you will simply lose it. Try to avoid using time off before you have earned it. If you quit before you have earned as much time as you have used, this may be deducted from your last paycheck.

401(k) plans are another common benefit, and often undervalued and misunderstood by women. A 401(k) plan is a retirement fund in which you invest money and your company will match your investment, sometimes by 50 to 100 percent. This is a benefit you can't afford not to understand and take advantage of. You are being paid to save money for your retirement, so ask human resources personnel what your company's plan includes.

Companies with Great Benefits

Work/life perks can vary based on size of company, geographic location, and, perhaps most importantly, the attitudes of senior management toward supporting and rewarding their employees. Here's a thumbnail sketch of some of the phenomenal employee benefits programs offered by top employers with exceptional offerings that can truly impact the lives of their employees. It's important to note first and foremost that all of these companies have comprehensive medical coverage and financial savings programs. That's important to recognize because a free exercise class isn't impressive if you don't have health insurance.

- **American Express.** The credit card giant offers a paid sabbatical program that allows employees with ten years of service to apply to take a paid leave of absence to perform community service for an average of three months.

- **NYU Medical Center.** One of the country's top teaching hospitals puts the talent of the world's best doctors and healthcare providers to use daily to support their employees with a comprehensive health and wellness program that includes programs such as walking clubs, early disease detection screenings, yoga courses, stress management seminars, and clinics on coping with cancer.

- **Pfizer.** The pharmaceutical leader will assist employees with the high cost of starting a family by reimbursing qualified adoption expenses up to $10,000 per child. In their outstanding commitment to community, Pfizer encourages philanthropy among employees by offering a very generous dollar for dollar match on charitable contributions up to $15,000 annually.

- **Viacom.** The media conglomerate that owns everything from CBS to MTV provides employees with an array of benefits as eclectic as their programming. New York–based staffers enjoy convenience and savings through subsidized meals in a fun cafeteria known as The Lodge. They provide access to a college coach to assist with selection and financing options for employees and their children, and the company's medical coverage includes generous fertility assistance, an area where others have cut back dramatically.

- **Citigroup.** This financial powerhouse makes emergency back-up childcare available to more employees than any other company in the world. They also offer subsidized full-time childcare.

- **Ernst & Young.** One of the world's largest accounting firms offers paid paternity leave so dads can bond with babies and provide moms with extra help at home.

RELOCATION NEGOTIATION

Moving is expensive. If you are moving on behalf of an employer, you may be the recipient of relocation benefits. Relocation benefits may cover moving costs, temporary housing costs, assistance in finding your spouse a new job in the area, assistance in selling your house, and possibly travel costs for return trips home if you relocate before your family does.

Larger companies are more likely to offer relocation benefits and to have a set relocation package. You can still negotiate according to your needs.

- **Make a list of what you would like help with.** Maybe you need help finding a good school for your children, or want the company to cover some of the costs of childcare.

- **Take into consideration changes in the cost of living.** You may want to ask for an increase to make up the difference.

- **Develop a relocation package tailored to your needs.** Make note of what you are willing to give up from the company's traditional package. Keep in mind your most important needs.

- **Evaluate how your package benefits the company.** For example, if they are willing to cover childcare costs temporarily, you will be able to start working sooner and be able to work longer hours. You are more likely to get your requests if you can design a plan that benefits the company as well.

- **Get your package in writing.** Just because your home office agrees to the package does not mean that your new office will.

- **Ask for a signing bonus.** If they are unwilling to deviate from their standard location package, a bonus can cover some of the remaining costs. Ask for it grossed up as well.

- **Ask if there's a repayment plan if you change jobs or if employment is terminated.** You may have to repay the company for the relocation costs if you leave the company before a specified length of time.

TUITION REIMBURSEMENT

Tuition reimbursement can be a very valuable benefit if you are planning to go back to school. Companies' tuition assistance programs vary widely, in how much they will reimburse, when you will be eligible, and what programs qualify for reimbursement. To understand your tuition reimbursement benefits, ask the right questions.

- How long must I work with the company before I qualify?

- How do I take advantage of the benefit?

- What kinds of programs will the company reimburse me for?

- What is covered under the policy, such as books or registration fees?

- Do continuing education courses qualify for tuition reimbursement?

- Do I need to get prior approval to take advantage of the program?

- How far in advance do I have to ask for tuition reimbursement?

- How many credits can I be reimbursed for?

- Does tuition reimbursement depend on my grades?

- How much will I be reimbursed?

- When will I be reimbursed?

- Is there a monetary ceiling to my tuition reimbursement dollars?

- Is there anything else I need to know?

In addition to tuition reimbursement, many companies offer scholarships for employees or their families. Ask your human resource department what is available and how to apply.

FLEXIBLE SCHEDULE

A flexible schedule means different things to different people. It can mean working from home or telecommuting, job-sharing, setting your own hours, or working part-time. Flexible schedule benefits are not usually offered by most companies, and will take skillful negotiation on your part. In addition to showing how a flexible schedule can benefit the company, you must be able to address all of their concerns. Your flexible schedule must make sense—to you and your employer.

- **Design a detailed plan.** When do you want to begin your new schedule? Why do you want to change your current schedule? What does your schedule entail? What days and times will you be in the office? What duties will you complete at home? What materials or setup will you need? How much will your plan cost?

- **List the concerns your employer is likely to have.** They will want to know if you are willing to come in for meetings and emergencies, how you will communicate with your other co-workers, and how efficient you will be under the new circumstances. Articulate how each concern will be addressed. Explain why you will be more efficient under your new schedule.

- **Make sure you can fulfill your part of the agreement.** Make sure you have the necessary tools and resources that will enable you to do your job remotely.

- **Consider the changes.** Discuss with your employer how your new schedule would affect your benefits, raises, or consideration for promotions and project assignments.

- **Compromise.** If your initial proposal is rejected, ask what parts you need to revise in order for it to be accepted.

MATERNITY LEAVE

Federal law protects women so that they can take up to twelve weeks of maternity leave without losing their position in the company, under the Family Medical Leave Act (FMLA). This law does not require companies to continue paying your salary during this time, but some companies offer the benefit of paid maternity leave. Read your company's maternity leave plan, or ask your human resources department for details. Sometimes you will not be eligible for paid leave but may still qualify for other company benefits. Ask whether FMLA time runs concurrently with the company's maternity leave and check your state's policy as well.

- **Tell your boss as soon as possible.** Seek the advice of your doctor as to when you should announce your pregnancy. Depending on your medical situation, it may be wise to wait until after the first trimester of pregnancy. Tell your boss before you confide in other coworkers, so she doesn't hear it through other sources. Communicate that you are dedicated to your position, and plan to work through your due date barring unforeseen circumstances.

- **Review your finances.** If you receive paid maternity leave, by all means use as much as you want. If you will not receive as much leave as you want to take, consider using vacation time or other personal leave. You could also think about working part-time for a period, or working from home to secure an income while you spend time with your baby.

- **Do not undervalue the importance of paid maternity leave as a benefit.** Maternity leave can affect your retirement benefits. Some companies will require you to work a certain number of hours in a year, for several years, before you qualify for pension benefits. For example, a company may require you to work for one thousand hours a year for five years before you qualify for its pension program. Maternity leave can keep you from completing the one thousand hours, pushing your pension benefits back a year. If you're unsure of how your company calculates this time, ask your HR representative.

Severance Packages

Severance packages can be difficult to negotiate because the conversation often takes place under less-than-ideal circumstances.

- When companies downsize a large group of people at once, some state and federal laws require giving employees advance notice. There may be a period when you are not required to report to work, but will continue receiving your wages and benefits. This, technically, is not a severance package but pay in lieu of notice. Severance is not required by law.

- Severance pay is extra pay you receive when you lose your job at no fault of your own, and the amount is usually based on the length of your employment. You may receive one week of pay or more depending on your company's policy for every year you worked at the company.

- In addition to severance pay, you may receive any unused vacation time, sick leave, and other acquired leave.

- Depending on your state's policy, severance pay may delay any unemployment income you apply for.

- Ask about COBRA (Consolidated Omnibus Reconciliation Act) procedures for your company, and if there will be any delays in your health benefits due to processing COBRA paperwork. COBRA provides continuation of group health coverage that otherwise would be terminated; however, this is at your expense.

- Severance pay can be paid in one lump sum or increments depending on company policy. It is to your advantage to ask for it in increments, as it may mean less tax will be taken out of your checks.

Some companies offer outplacement services as part of the severance package. These services won't necessarily find you a job, but will help you with confidence, résumé writing, interviewing techniques, and other job-searching skills. They may also provide access to computers, printers, phones, fax machines, and job listings. Use them.

PREPARING FOR EVALUATIONS

Many companies have regularly scheduled employee evaluations. If your employer does not, it may be beneficial to request one. You'll treat it with the same level of importance as you would a salary negotiation as we discussed earlier in this chapter.

- **Bring all documents requested.** Also bring any materials you would like to show to support your opinions. Bring a pen and paper to take notes.

- **Think about what you would like to discuss.** Now is the time to bring up any suggestions you have about changes for the office and changes for your position. What would you like to add to your job responsibilities? Would you like a raise or a promotion? Arm yourself with plenty of examples of your successes to justify your requests.

- **Practice what you plan to say.** It will help you to communicate all of your ideas. You will be less likely to forget something and will sound clearer and more professional.

- **Know your strengths and how you would like to channel them.** Make a career route for how you'd like to grow with the company and tell the manager in the evaluation. You are more likely to get something if you ask for it. Your manager can tell you exactly what you will need to do to get what you want.

- **Honestly think about your weaknesses.** They will more than likely come up, so it is better to be prepared. If you are not taken by surprise, you can offer a plan as to how you will overcome your deficit. Your manager will be impressed that you had the integrity to admit to your own weaknesses, and then the willingness to improve them. Ask to take a continuing education course, a seminar, or workshop, or simply have a good explanation ready of how you will do things differently in the future. Managers don't like excuses, so don't challenge their opinions unless you are truly justified.

- **Stay in control of your emotions at all times.** No matter what is said to you, try not to cry or overreact to something. Think before you speak and don't worry about creating pauses in conversation.

GET THE RAISE YOU DESERVE

Many people are afraid to ask for a raise, but this is a fear you must get over fast. Know your boss's expectations regarding your performance and if you're sure you've met them, ask for a raise. Raises rarely fall into your lap. You know you deserve it. You've put in long hours and extra effort, often at personal sacrifices. Don't let your hard work go unnoticed and unrewarded.

- **Know your company's salary increase policies.** You may only be eligible for a raise after you have worked for a company for a certain time, if you work full-time, only during your reviews and evaluations, or other limitations. You may only be eligible for a certain percentage increase. Knowing this information will prevent you from asking for a raise you probably won't receive.

- **Compile a list of your achievements.** Researching for a raise is an all-year job. Keep a running list of your most impressive accomplishments. Did you absorb more job responsibilities? What has changed since your last salary increase? What are your greatest successes? When nobody else could get the job done, how did you rise to the occasion?

- **Research.** As you did when negotiating your initial salary, research the salaries of similar professionals in similar companies.

- **Consider the timing.** Try to ask for a raise after you have just finished a major project successfully.

- **Schedule a time to speak with your boss.** It is important to consider her schedule and choose a time when you are least likely to be interrupted. Do not ask for a raise in a spontaneous meeting. You do not want to put her on the spot or catch her at a bad time. She will need time to prepare for the meeting just as you did.

- **Consider compensation besides salary.** If your company had a rocky quarter financially, ask for increased benefits, a new office, or vacation time instead of a salary increase.

- **Think about the right approach to take.** If your boss is a no-nonsense person, keep your request short, direct, and to the point. If she is more intuitive, state your reasons and how you thought things through.

- **Think about what your boss will value.** If they could care less about the monthly newsletter, do not submit your contribution to the monthly newsletter as your criteria for deserving a raise.

If she says no, all is not lost. Ask her to identify areas for development and what you need to work on before you qualify for a raise. Ask when you can schedule another evaluation. If you were declined for reasons out of her hands, ask when the circumstances will change.

As we've discussed in this chapter, the most important elements of any successful negotiation are a willingness on your part to participate in such conversations using the knowledge and confidence you've gained through solid research. Never again should you simply accept what's been offered without giving consideration to the possibility of negotiating. Even though not everything will be negotiable, you must be comfortable with the prospect of partaking in the process. Stand up for what you believe you deserve and don't sell yourself short.

CHAPTER ELEVEN

• • •

Maintain Your After Hours
Finding Balance From 9 to 5, and Beyond

"Women want men, careers, money, children, friends, luxury, comfort, independence, freedom, respect, love, and $3 pantyhose that won't run."

—PHYLLIS DILLER

It's 5:55 P.M. You've still got to put the finishing touches on tomorrow morning's presentation. Daycare closes at 6:30 and there's nobody else to pick up the kids. Dinner's still in the freezer and the dry-cleaning's been ready to be picked up for a week. Tickets for tonight's symphony concert are on the refrigerator, but the baby-sitter hasn't confirmed with you. Yikes—all you want to do is scream.

How many different roles are you juggling: career woman, wife, mother, daughter, companion, friend, homemaker, shopper, cook, confidante, housekeeper, errand runner, volunteer, chauffeur, and more? It's exhausting just thinking about the many jobs we have.

Perhaps like many women, you've noticed that there just aren't enough hours in the day to satisfy the requirements of all those jobs and still find time to relax. Every woman who has tried knows you can't keep all the balls in the air, at least not all at the same time. Your goal is to prioritize, organize, and learn to balance life's demands. Whether you're single, married, divorced, partnered, living with a roommate, raising kids, or empty nesting, you'll find ideas here that will help you achieve the balance you're searching for and ways to manage a full plate in spite of the challenges.

Are You Running on Empty?

Just like your car, you can only go so far on a tank of fuel. You speed along, doing everything in sight, meeting the needs of everyone in your circle of family and friends, and then *whammo,* all of a sudden you're out of gas and you don't know how it happened. There's no need to crash and burn in your effort to juggle a million things. You're obviously competent and capable or you wouldn't even be *trying* to do it all—and nobody expects you to be able to do it alone and seamlessly. Since there's no "full" or "empty" gauge on your life, you must find the shortcuts that will let you use your energy most efficiently.

"When I had my daughter Hannah, I was the VP of global advertising at a major fragrance company," says Marisa Thalberg. "I attended a local New Mommies luncheon and was surprised when I found that most of the women there were not returning to work. When I did return to work a few weeks later, I tried to hang on to a group playdate with some of the women I met, even convincing several of them to wait till late Friday afternoon when I could swing it. But that timing didn't last, and once there, I was amazed at how divergent our topics of conversation had become."

Thalberg soon realized she wasn't striving so much to achieve some kind of "balance" as she was simply looking to feel a sense of connection with other women whose lives resembled hers. "What I really needed most was to share stories, laugh, and commiserate over the big juggle," she says. "My need was so great that, ironically, to solve it I saddled myself with a second career, and launched Executive Moms (executivemoms.com). Now, through my own experiences as well as through the lens of hundreds of other 'Executive Moms,' I have a lot of perspective on work and family."

As the Founder of Executive Moms, Thalberg offers these observations:

- "Life consists of choices, and your goal should be to find a total picture in which, overall, the compromises are acceptable and the benefits are strong. For instance, my husband and I make our lives as dual-career parents work by living in an apartment in New York City, so we avoid a long commute. For us, that has been more important than enjoying the space of a nice house in the suburbs.

- "Discuss with your employer how much you also value your role as a mother, and seek some flexibility (even if it means just being able to scoot out occasionally for a school event) so that you feel like you are being true to both.

- "Know your kids will be no less smart, talented, successful, and loving of you than the kids who have their mothers home with them all day. As they grow, have lives of their own, and look for adult role models, you'll probably be their biggest."

Take Back Your Time

There are basics to your life: you get up, get dressed, eat breakfast (well, maybe), do your chores and if there are kids, pets, or significant others, you manage their mornings, too. Then it's off to the "real" world for a day of stress and toil. Back to the mommy track or the part of your life that's really real until bedtime. How do some women do it and never seem frazzled? Chances are they're every bit as stressed as you are; they've just either found ways to hide it *or* ways to reduce the stress by making important choices that allow them to live the way they want. You can do it, too, with some self-analysis, simple changes, and a great attitude that says "Hey, I'm important and I want my life back."

MICROMANAGE ONE DAY

Have you ever tried to start a diet by keeping a food diary? Were you surprised at how much you actually ate during a day when you thought you were being "good"? It's important to take a snapshot of your daily behavior to get a true picture of your life, and not just with food. You probably don't realize half of what you accomplish every day. For a single day, write down everything you do and how much time you devote to it. The idea is to focus on a clear picture of your schedule and how you spend your time. Nobody's judging you, and there's no right or wrong.

You'll want to include everything from wake-up to bedtime. As you review your notes, consider things you could have skipped or that other people could have done. Do you feel like you wasted time on unnecessary activities? Even if you think every minute was time well spent, we're going to help you find ways to shave precious moments off of your most mundane chores to give you time for yourself.

SIX STEPS TO A BALANCED LIFE

The following steps are suggestions for reclaiming your life. That doesn't mean it will be smooth sailing from this point on, but if you pay attention to that inner voice, the one that says slow down, you move too fast, you'll make a little progress at a time.

1. **Do the most important things first.** And then do what is possible. Even Superwoman can't be in two places at once. Set short-term goals based on daily or weekly priorities. Make every effort to achieve those tasks and don't waste time feeling guilty for missing a meeting or a baseball game.

2. **Let yourself have a bad day now and then.** Even Barbara Walters gets runs in her hose. Learn to let go of the little stuff and you'll have room for the important things. Mistakes happen.

3. **A television set has an OFF switch and you need one, too.** There's no rule that says you have to answer the phone every time it rings. Instead of being distracted by every call, use technology to your advantage. Indulge yourself with caller ID and voice mail to manage calls effectively.

4. Learn to say "so what!" The grass needs mowing, the windows are streaky, and you haven't washed the car in weeks. Big deal. Give yourself a break on the things that don't really matter.

5. Learn to say "NO" and mean it. Sure, the charity bazaar is for a good cause. But so is spending time with your kids. No, you really don't want to chair the membership committee for your church. Membership in your family is all you can handle right now. No, you don't want to attend the convention. It would be good for your career, but you have family commitments, too, and there will be another convention next year, and the year after, and the year after that.

6. Control the controllables. Let the stuff that's not in your control take its course. And at the end of the day, hug your kids, kiss your partner, call your mom and pat yourself on the back for making it through another twenty-four hours. Take one day at a time.

PICK YOUR PASSIONS

Decide what's really important to you, then try to prioritize your responsibilities. For instance, is it more important to serve gourmet home-cooked meals than to take an evening yoga class? Which matters more: nightly phone chats with friends or a neat pantry?

Ask yourself what can you afford to give up in your quest for balance. What can you delegate to others? How can you make your job work for you, rather than against you?

● **Don't put off paying bills or doing unpleasant chores.** Group chores so that you can accomplish several at once. For example, arrange to pay your bills online on the same day each month. Allow enough time to complete the tasks at hand. Most people underestimate how long a task will take, and that leads to frustration and defeat, both of which are negative feelings that undermine your accomplishments.

BOOK BREAK

Journalist and politico Maria Shriver turned a commencement speech at the College of the Holy Cross into a short book that's filled with encouraging and entertaining lessons. In *Ten Things I Wish I'd Known Before I Went Out Into the Real World* (Warner Books, 2000), Shriver reveals surprising and humorous anecdotes about her marriage, career, and motherhood in a friendly and inspiring style. It's fun to read, but even more enjoyable in the audio version, since it's like listening to the very likeable Shriver talk directly to you.

• **Stick to a task until it's complete.** Having to reorient yourself to a partially completed job wastes time and can lead to errors as well. Procrastination is not a good policy.

• **Delegate responsibility.** Get family members or hired help such as a baby-sitter, assistant, or housekeeper to take on some of the burdens. Even if you're feeling strapped for cash, it's sometimes more efficient to hire a student for $5 or $10 per hour to run errands and handle chores to free up your time for more lucrative needs.

SURVIVAL TRICKS FOR THE OVERWORKED

Have you got your company convinced you are absolutely essential and that you're at their beck and call 24/7? The really savvy worker will figure out how to let her company know she's all theirs, but that she's her own gal, too. You may not get your supervisors to agree to all of these concessions, but with a strong argument, the courage of your convictions, and the support of others, you may find yourself forging the way into a new concept of the workplace—one that feeds workers' spirits as well as their bank accounts. After all, showing up rested, contented with your life, and secure about your family will help increase the quality of your work immeasurably. So ask. Do it diplomatically, in a spirit of sharing rather than confrontation, and be ready to back up your requests with good reasons why it will work for both you and them.

• **Ask for flextime.** Perhaps if you can work ten hours a day for four days a week, you can have an entire day off for yourself, and still give the company the same number of hours.

- **Job share.** If you don't need to work full-time, share the job with someone else. Divide the time and the responsibilities, but understand the implications to your salary and benefits.

- **Utilize onsite daycare.** More companies are becoming sensitive to parental needs. If the kids are nearby, Mom is less likely to call in sick or leave work to check on them.

- **Combine work and pleasure.** Take your family on out-of-town business trips. Add a weekend and turn it into a family getaway. This has the added advantage of saving money, since the company's paying for your travel and part of your expenses already.

- **Ask about telecommuting.** Think of the hours you can save working from home, even just part of the time. One word of caution: Be sure you are disciplined enough to actually work when you're home. You don't want to jeopardize your job by watching soap operas instead of doing your work.

- **Buy back hours.** If the money's not the issue, try negotiating with your company for extra time off, paid back at your hourly or weekly rate.

IT WORKS FOR ME

Clear out the clutter

St. Louis–based executive assistant Mary Kay Chapel wins rave reviews for organization and efficiency. Among her top tips: "Organize your desk in a manner that eliminates the need to get up and down. Have needed supplies and often-used files at a hand's reach. Always file as you go. The contents of 'To Be Filed' folders never get filed. Delete unwanted emails. Shred documents if you don't ever need to look at them again. Instead of allowing them to pile up, add new phone numbers to your Rolodex® daily."

GIVE ME JUST A LITTLE MORE TIME

Here are some strategies to help shave minutes and hours from tedious routines while freeing up the time for better use.

- **Keep a master calendar by the phone.** If you keep more than one calendar (in your computer, at work, on your desk) be sure to update daily to all the others.

- **Use Post-it notes to give yourself reminders.** Stick them on your handbag, computer screen, and even in the car to help you remember the day's important "to-dos."

- **Write things down wherever you are.** Keep a notepad or index cards with you at all times—in your purse, pocket, desk, and next to the bed. When you think of something you have to do, jot it down. Make a habit of checking the cards at the end of each day, and adding the information to your calendar or lists as appropriate.

- **Fall in love with lists.** Several types of lists can really help to organize your life. A daily to-do list is crucial—don't go to bed without checking this list. If you don't get everything accomplished, add leftovers to tomorrow's list. A weekly calendar or a monthly master schedule will keep mid-range goals in mind. And a six- or twelve-month list with recurring events (like appointments with the doctor and dentist, license renewals, and tax deadlines) helps keep important dates in your memory.

There are still plenty of ways to squeeze extra minutes out of your busy schedule in all areas of your life, which often helps ease the burden of juggling a jam-packed work and home life.

- **Be a savvy shopper.** Shop in bulk, but check prices. Large sizes aren't always a bargain. Stock up on staples for the house and the kitchen—but make sure you have space to store your purchases. Organize your coupons before you go to the store. Shop from catalogs or the Internet for items whose quality you trust. You can often get free shipping, save sales tax, and avoid long trips to the mall.

- **Plan ahead.** Buy a special date book with birthdays, anniversaries, and other dates to remember every year. Make a monthly or even an annual visit to the card shop with this book and buy your cards at one time. Address and stamp them to be sent out at the appropriate time. Alternatively, sign up with an online reminder service that will send you an email notifying you of upcoming dates to remember.

- **Delegate.** Involve the whole family in household chores. Even the littlest kids can be taught to put their things away.

- **Multitask.** You do it at work so you can do it at home. If you don't have a cordless or cell phone consider getting a hands-free phone with a headset. You can return calls while you're cooking or waiting in the carpool line or stuck in a massive traffic jam on the highway (but not while the car is moving, of course).

- **Eat right.** What you eat and when you eat it often affects your mood throughout the day. Be smart about the choices that are best for you. Take vitamins based on your doctor's advice to support your good nutrition.

- **Exercise.** To perform best at work, you've got to feel your best and exercise is often the answer. This doesn't have to be at a gym. Meet a friend and walk in the park or at the mall. Take the family for a bike ride or a hike. Park in the last space at the grocery store. Use these "slice of life" exercises to supplement regular workouts.

- **Get enough sleep.** Fatigue causes you to be less energetic, less efficient, and deprives you of enjoying your waking hours to the fullest.

- **Learn to play.** Since all work and no play makes anyone a dull girl, having a focused activity during leisure time is not wasting time; it's giving you something to look forward to and helps reduce stress.

- **Indulge yourself.** Have a manicure, a pedicure, eat chocolate, or buy yourself an item of clothing you've been coveting.

LOVE SMART

Healthy relationships make for a more balanced person. To be your best on the job, it helps to have a solid support system out of the office. Make time to be alone with your partner, and make time for your kids, separately and together. Keep the lines of communication open and have a buddy you can talk openly to about anything.

Relish the Time You've Saved

 IT WORKS FOR ME ···

Make a play date

Jill Murphy Long, author of *Permission to Play: Taking Time to Renew Your Smile* (Sourcebooks, 2003), encourages women to find "me time" without guilt or delay: "Write 'meeting' on your calendar and take yourself out for a quiet lunch, get a massage, or have a cup of tea. Learn to say, 'I am in a very important meeting—with me—I deserve this time alone to ponder, to sit, and to just relax.'

"Ask for support. You might be inclined to cancel your appointment with yourself, but if you have committed this time to meet with someone else, you just might get there more regularly. Book an hour with a friend to walk or Rollerblade after work. Start a fitness program with an associate or a personal trainer to get you on track and in the habit.

"Another way to make a commitment is to sign up for a worthy cause: Run your first marathon for leukemia research or do a three-day walk to increase awareness about breast cancer prevention. Pick a 5K race, writing contest, or art show to enter in a year from now. Make this time for yourself and in return, you will be giving back to others."

* * *

But what if you still haven't learned how to manage a full plate, play, slow down, and take time for yourself? What happens to the woman who can't say no, who gets anxiety attacks if she misses a single activity or can't fulfill every request that comes her way? What happens to the woman who can't stop to hear her family say they need her because she is so preoccupied?

At best, she does a halfhearted job at most things, does one or two well, and ignores a bunch more. At worst, she burns out, consumed by guilt, anxiety, and stress. She sends the wrong email to the wrong client, she miscalculates the budget, she forgets a crucial meeting, or she snaps at her co-workers and alienates her boss.

If you ate a hot dog, slice of pizza, and an ice-cream sundae all in one sitting, you'd feel sick. Your body can only take so much—even of the good stuff. The same applies to your work/life balance. Don't run yourself ragged. Slow down and take it step by step. Do what you can, but remember to keep yourself and your physical and emotional health at the top of the priorities list.

So, what's the bottom line? Look back at what you've learned and try to implement even one idea today. You can't teach an old dog new tricks instantly, so don't try to make dramatic changes all at one time. Take it one step at a time—and stick to it—and we know the rewards will follow.

CHAPTER TWELVE

Cultivate a Peanut Gallery
Friends and Mentors Can Champion Your Success

"Surround yourself only with people who are going to lift you higher."
—OPRAH WINFREY

Oprah has Gayle, her best friend and sidekick, who she knows will always give it to her straight. In addition to shopping, gossiping, and doing other girl stuff, they're also able to love, laugh, and cry together. They know each other's secrets, strengths, and foibles—and they adore each other anyway.

It's rare for any of us to thrive on our own. Not just the need for intimate partners or romance; this is about a solid support system to aid the personal and professional life of a career woman like you. The most successful women have identified and developed such circles to aid their success. Regardless of your income level or field, it's important to have a best friend, mentor, and role model. Sometimes it's one person who fills all three roles; for other women it's many.

Just as working moms must provide emergency contact numbers for their children's school records, we want you to identify who you'd call for personal and professional crises and support for yourself. Throughout this chapter we'll share lessons that prove the power of friendship and guidance in contributing to your overall happiness and success.

Friends

"Friendship with one's self is all important, because without it one cannot be friends with anyone else in the world."
—ELEANOR ROOSEVELT

As women we love to celebrate our friends. We throw engagement parties to root for marital bliss. We give baby showers, replete with as much advice as cake and punch. We pass on our baby clothes along with precious memories. TV personality Star Jones took a bunch of pals to Montego Bay, Jamaica, for a girls-only birthday bash to ring in her fortieth.

Since the dawn of time, women have formed a circle of support for times of crisis, transition, joy, and sorrow. If you're out of town, you have someone to feed the pets and water the plants. If your heart is broken, you know just who to call for comfort. You've got a list of servicepeople for your home, car, and office. Even your computer has a backup system in case of a crash, but who do you have when your career is in dire need of help?

Your best friends and confidantes need not be female. Your best friend might be your husband, boyfriend or significant other. Not only might he or she be an effective sounding board to provide solid career advice, your partner could be the one to help you on a daily basis to implement the advice you receive from others. You don't want a "yes" person, but someone who is willing to lay it on the line—the good, the bad, and the ugly.

 IT WORKS FOR ME

Healthy mom/daughter dynamic yields career success

"As a mother of two daughters, my biggest pleasure is to be their most ardent fan. From watching their tennis matches and swim meets as youngsters to witnessing their development to wonderful women, I've loved being their loudest cheerleader. Even though I've never looked for anything from them, to my surprise our relationship has served as the greatest source of strength and determination for me personally and professionally. Our bond goes full circle: I steadfastly encourage them to follow their passions and, in turn, their happiness and success fuels my desire to pursue my own professional dreams as well. Julie, Liz, and I lovingly push each other to achieve our very best." —Nancy Stein, an entrepreneur in Ambler, PA

Some of the ways women bond with each other include book clubs, card games, slumber parties, meals, gossip, exercise classes, childbirth classes, and their kids' activities. If you nurture those ties to keep them strong and healthy, then there's a good chance they would prove to be the career lifeline you need someday. Your Scrabble buddy might not only be gifted at coming up with seven-letter words, she could also score big by offering you exceptional professional advice. When in need of help, your personal friendships should be viewed as a goldmine.

Mentors

Sometimes you need more than a friend—someone to offer more than a kind word and a hug. You need an expert with specific information, life experience, and advice that will help you move forward. That's when you need a mentor. She is a counselor, guide, leader, and pinup picture on your calendar of success. Chances are you fit into one of these categories:

- **Eye on the prize.** You know just what you want, but you need the help of others to reach the goal.

- **Still in school or just out and looking for a job.** You really don't know just what you want to do. Talking with more experienced women can help you set your course and possibly avoid sidetracks, which can come in the form of years spent in a field or job that's not suited to your personality or goals.

- **The single-track gal.** You started in a field and you may have advanced, but you're tired and afraid that you've been pigeon-holed. You wonder if you're able to do anything else or if you'll be taken seriously. You'll enjoy chapter 3 on reinventing yourself. It'll be important to identify people who can help you start off on the right foot to a new career. Or they can help you find the right path to continue in your current direction, but in fresh, dynamic ways.

- **I don't know what I want to be.** You've tried it all, but haven't found just what you want. Nothing quite fits your talents and de-sires and you don't know where to turn. You definitely need to get to know some successful, motivated women who can inspire you and help you sort out the dreams from the real possibilities.

In our first book, *Women For Hire: The Ultimate Guide to Getting a Job,* we outlined steps for finding a mentor. Briefly, these include:

1. Start with a clear focus. What do you need right now?

2. List the people you admire professionally.

3. Interview prospective mentors.

4. Be clear about what you are asking in time commitments and expectations.

5. Remember that mentoring is a two-way street. Both of you must benefit.

But how do you go about looking for a mentor? Here are some places to start your search.

- **Know yourself.** Know what you're looking for before you expect someone else to help in the search. You'll increase your self-awareness through the process, but have a general idea ahead of time where you think you want to go.

- **Talk to people.** Anyone can be a mentor, just as anyone can help you find one. Talk to parents, friends, coworkers, clergy. Sometimes this kind of talk turns into a mentoring relationship, but more often it leads to finding others better suited to help you.

- **Go back to chapter 6 and read about making contacts.** Work that list for all it's worth. Ask for referrals and names.

- **Talk to your company.** Savvy corporations set up mentoring programs to develop their talent. If they have such a program, you may benefit from it. If they don't, you might get points for making the suggestion. This can be a marvelous low-cost or no-cost benefit for the company to offer.

- **Contact role models you read about in newspapers, magazines, and books.** Be polite, state what you're looking for. Many "famous" people had mentors themselves and will be glad to work with you, even on a limited basis. It can't hurt to try.

- **Use your connections.** Check out your high school or college alumni organization. Get active in it. Check with teachers and professors to see if they can help you get in touch with a prospective mentor. That "old school tie" is a strong bond when you're looking for advice.

- **Look at contacts from your old jobs.** They know you, your skills, and your value. As long as you left on good terms, these people can be valuable assets.

- **Look for mentors among your peers.** Mentors don't have to have executive titles or strings of degrees after their names. They have to be someone who can further your career ambitions. Don't be a snob . . . use anyone and everyone you can find.

- **Use your human resources department.** Have a chat with your company's HR professional—not as a mentor, but as a facilitator to get you together with a good one.

- **Retired executives often love to stay in touch by mentoring rising stars.** Let them help your light shine. They've got a wealth of experience and insight to share.

- **Investigate professional organizations.** Many local and national groups have both formal and informal programs.

- **Read professional journals and magazines.** Initiate a correspondence with someone whose words grab your attention. Show your interest in her and she may reciprocate.

- **Contact people who have helped you in the past.** They don't have to be high-powered business executives. You never know who's going to have the magic to lift you to the next level.

- **Rent a mentor.** If all else fails, or if your situation is truly unique, you may choose to invest in a professional counseling program to help jump-start or invigorate your journey along the career path.

NO ONE DOES IT ALONE

"The most important sign of success is personal dignity. Real personal success is not measured by money or fame. In fact, you could have very little money, no fame, and be hugely successful," says Greta Van Susteren, anchor of Fox News Channel's *On the Record with Greta Van Susteren*.

"Less important is career success, which is fun and challenging but certainly not the most important thing in life. I've worked hard and deserve some credit for my success, but I was hugely fortunate to have others helping me in all sorts of ways. I've never been so foolish to think I was doing this all alone."

Van Susteren grew up in the '50s and '60s, when women were told they couldn't pursue certain careers. At home, however, she says her parents taught her otherwise. "They made it plain to me that I could do whatever I wanted and that they'd help me.

"I went on to college and then law school, but career success demands more than simply gathering diplomas. I spent many years trying cases and working around the clock—getting dirt under my fingernails.

Along the way, I collected friends who inspired and taught me. Meeting my husband, also a lawyer, a few months out of law school enhanced my career and my life. From November 1979 when he hired me to do legal research until now, we've continued to share the highs and the lows, and at all times support each other. I enjoy his successes and he enjoys mine."

When she jumped to the media arena, Van Susteren credits mentors such as Gail Evans, former executive vice president of CNN, with guiding her through the perilous waters of cable news. "She watched my back, and gave me candid advice. She was smart enough to give good advice and I was smart enough to follow it.

"When I moved on from CNN to FOX, I discovered more great allies. Just as with prior jobs, I managed to find the best people who are interested in joint success. It's much easier to do a good job when the environment is one in which people are excited about their work.

"Even with the career change, at all times, I turned to my best friend—my husband. We have never stopped talking since we met in 1979."

Is there a secret to success? Yes, claims Van Susteren. "Make very good friends, listen to them, and never forget that your career success is not all your own creation. It is a group effort, and the group is forever changing. When you begin to think you've done it alone, you're in deep emotional trouble (and wrong!)."

3-2-1 CONTACT!

Congratulations to you! You found a person you'd like to have help you along, and she's agreed to support your efforts. So what's next?

First, you must define the relationship. Let her know what you want from her, why you want her help, and how you envision benefits for the both of you. (And by the way, there's no rule that says you are limited to a single mentor. You may find you want several people, at different times, or for different aspects of your career advancement.) Do your research to learn about her career path, and use this information in asking her to help you advance. Ask good questions and show you're interested in the answers.

Work together to set the ground rules. Here are a few things to consider:

- **How often will you meet?** Before you approach your mentor, have a good idea of how much time you'd like from her. Do you need to meet once a month or more?

- **Under what circumstances will you meet?** Coffeeshop, home, or office? Morning, lunch, evening, or weekends?

- **How will you stay in touch?** By phone or email? Ask what is easiest for her and be willing to accommodate that.

- **Confidentiality.** This is a must on both sides, especially if you work for the same company or know many of the same people professionally. You're likely to discuss work situations and professional relationships in the course of your work together, and you must agree to keep all information just between you.

- **Honesty.** If you can't exchange ideas freely there's no use in getting started.

- **Sensitivity.** Be willing to take constructive criticism, but be sensitive to each other's feelings at the same time.

- **Openness.** A closed mind wastes everybody's time.

- **Willingness to learn.** Isn't that what this is all about?

- **A no-fault escape clause.** If your personalities don't mesh or one of you finds you don't have the time to devote to this cause, agree ahead of time on a graceful, no-excuses-needed exit.

WHAT DO YOU GET FROM A MENTOR?

A mentor's not going to land you a cushy job. She may provide you with contacts to help, but her responsibilities are more personal and concrete.

- She's a role model—a success you're aiming to emulate. She can teach you business behavior and skills, from how to talk to clients to how to dress to impress.

- She's a fountain of information, from names of contacts for networking to certification and skills you should pursue.

- She's a sounding board, someone to hear your ideas and critique them honestly.

- She's a champion, ready to suggest you for promotion or a new job.

- She's a counselor, open to listening to your concerns and prepared to help you get past them.

- She's a caution, warning you of pitfalls and problems.

- She's a teacher, instructing you in the ways of your industry and the business world.

- She's an entree to other professionals in your chosen field. If you're lucky, she's an example for your personal and professional growth.

WHAT DO YOU BRING TO THE TABLE?

The mentoring process isn't like a mother bird dropping worms into a baby's mouth to provide all its nourishment. You'll need to be open and receptive, and ready to work for the benefits you expect to gain.

Before you start, make your goals and objectives clear. Be flexible because they are likely to change, but you don't want to waste a mentor's time by making her dredge your ideas out of you. Be willing to listen, and be ready to share willingly with your mentor. Your admiration will be a plus for her, your honest assessment of her help for you will be an aid for her future mentoring.

Be positive. Enter the mentor relationship convinced that it will be good for both of you. If you go into it doubting the purpose, you may as well stay home.

BOOK BREAK

CNN anchor Soledad O'Brien credits two top picks for helping to advance her career:

Be Your Own Mentor: Strategies from Top Women on the Secrets of Success, by Sheila Wellington (Random House, 2001) because "it's not always possible to find mentors at every stage in your career. Women are naturally nurturing so be supportive of yourself and mentor yourself. This advice has helped me in a variety of situations."

In *Having It All: Black Women and the Question of Success* (Doubleday, 2003), author Veronica Chambers "gives sound advice for women of color who are looking to manage a successful career, have a great relationship, and a happy, healthy family." She focuses on "how hard it is to accomplish all of these things, but with hard work it really is possible."

And most important of all, be considerate. Don't waste your time or hers. Be punctual, friendly but not chatty or gossipy, and give the session your entire concentration. Be aware that mentorship is a two-way relationship. What will your mentor get from you? Several things:

• You can offer her valuable feedback on her own career.

• She'll gain skills as a listener and a teacher.

• She'll learn from your experiences and pass those things on to others.

• You'll give her a new perspective on the company or industry as a whole.

Sometimes the person who provides you with exceptional inspiration doesn't even know your name. Role models are usually professionals whom we look up to—we follow their careers and we admire their success. We might even long to be just like them.

Aspiring journalists often cite superstars Barbara Walters, Diane Sawyer, and Katie Couric as their role models. These three ladies of network news pave the way for generations of talent and they inspire legions of women both in the television industry and out. They do this by being the best in their business and by giving speeches and interviews that are accessed by their fans. Similarly, by becoming the first American woman in space, Sally Ride's strides led other women to dream big and to reach for the stars in their own chosen profession.

You can learn a lot from women you don't know personally. Study their paths and research their backgrounds to find clues to their success. As you advance in your career, remember that your advice and experiences are valuable to others. Be willing to return the favor and lend a hand because it's the best way to build meaningful personal and professional relationships.

CONCLUSION

· · ·

Cheers to Success

"Who knows? Somewhere out there in this audience may even be someone who will one day follow in my footsteps, and preside over the White House as the president's spouse. I wish him well."

— BARBARA BUSH,
in her commencement address to Wellesley College

The dictionary defines *success* as "the favorable or prosperous termination of attempts or endeavors; the attainment of wealth, position, honors or the like." We define success as getting where you want to be, being happy with your decisions and rewarded for those choices in both tangible and nontangible ways. It may not be easy and it may not be quick, but as the preceding chapters have shown you, it is possible to chart your own course and reach your goals. We know it can be done especially because there are millions of women just like you who've done it.

In this conclusion, we celebrate seemingly ordinary women just like the rest of us who've succeeded on their own terms. Even though they're all successful in a wide range of fields, this group shares one common bond: They're out-of-the-box thinkers and dreamers who haven't let fear or old-fashioned stereotypes keep them from reaching their goals. If they can do it, so can you. We promise. Let their lessons from the trenches inspire you.

I'm a Strong Negotiator

In the negotiation process it's okay to push back if you're not feeling completely comfortable with the way things are going. Ask questions and expect answers.

"Would you buy a house without doing an inspection or checking out the neighborhood?" asks Cynthia Stevens, an associate professor at the Robert H. Smith School of Business at the University of Maryland. "A lot of women are very concerned if the other party likes them. It is equally important to worry about whether or not the other person respects you. You're negotiating not just a salary, but also a relationship. If you are agreeable or submissive from the start in the negotiation process, who do you think they will go to with all the dirty work? Do you really want to be the only person who takes out the trash every day?"

I'm Always Ready for Surprise

"I responded to an ad for a position at a public relations firm. The process consisted of an oral interview, a typing test, and a surprise written press release test," says Patricia Froelich of Orlando-based PR/PR. "It turns out most of the interviewees had chickened out once they reached the written press release exam, but I stuck it out and wrote the best release I could. It must've worked because right away I was offered the position. I got this job because of my persistence and my refusal to give up even when faced with a potentially scary test."

I Asked for It

"About twenty years ago, the Society of Women Engineers offered a seminar on the Imposter Syndrome. There I learned that women frequently don't ask for promotions and other recognition. I was following the approach of waiting for recognition," says Betty Shanahan, executive director of Society of Women Engineers (www.swe.org) and herself an electrical engineer. "After this seminar, I always ask what goals I must reach to get promoted; ask for feedback when I believe I reach those goals; and ask for the promotion when I've completed the goals. Every promotion that I have received since then was because I asked for it."

I Use My Creativity

When advertising associate Robin Daniels wanted a long-overdue promotion, she sent a customized T-shirt with Batman and Robin on it to her boss—with her own face superimposed as Robin. She attached a note with the T-shirt that read, "Even Batman needs Robin. You'll be a superhero if you consider giving me the raise I deserve." She documented quantifiable reasons for the raise and yes, Bat-fans, she got it.

I See Red

To get the attention of a prospective public relations client, Susan Simonelli and her team sent a bubblegum machine filled with red gumballs. They included the company's well-researched proposal, similar case studies, and a client list with a handwritten note that read, "We're red-y to go to work on your behalf. We hope you'll choose us." The combination of a strong serious proposal and a touch of whimsy won them the account.

I Do My Homework

Magda Dvir arrived at an interview with five references who she knew her interviewer respected. She had researched everyone they could possibly know in common and got permission from each one to use them as a reference. The company was so impressed with her credentials and the network she had assembled that they hired her at the salary and terms she requested.

I Am Clever

A St. Louis writer wanted the attention of a newsletter publisher who was impossible to reach. To circumvent what felt like Pentagon-type barriers, she sent him a package with a helium balloon that was tied to a personalized letter. When he opened the box, the balloon floated up to reveal the note, "Hire Juliet O'Connor because I'll rise to every occasion." O'Connor included writing samples and bound them so her presentation was top-notch. She was floating on air when she learned that her creative delivery and excellent work landed her the job.

I Stay on My Own Turf

Michell Phelan wanted an exciting career in the high-profile entertainment industry—in Wyoming, of all places. Initially she thought she'd have to move elsewhere to pursue this dream. But through extensive research, she discovered the Wyoming Film Office, which encourages production companies to use the state for commercial and film locations. She started in a part-time role on *Starship Troopers*, and now manages the whole organization. Her days are logged by marketing film sites, coordinating production logistics, and assisting with crew and support services, all of which is a dream job that any aspiring or accomplished arts buff would envy. And as if that weren't enough, Phelan works with the likes of Robert Redford to boot.

I've Got the Right Package

These days it's not enough to meet only a portion of the job requirements. Employers look for the ideal overall package, which is the right mix of hard and soft skills. "I got the job because I was the most qualified technically and had the interpersonal and presentation skills to complement my technical ability," says Shannon R. Fuchs, member of a process control team at Chevron. "I got the promotion because I know how to work well with a cross-functional team to get things done, I'm flexible and willing to do whatever it takes to meet the needs of our business, and I took the roles that my peers passed on. This resulted in me having broader business knowledge and the experience necessary to be an effective manager."

I Promote My Transferable Skills

After traveling as a TV reporter throughout the country, Nicole L'Huillier returned home to Vermont in hopes of switching gears to public relations. She knew that her newsroom experience could serve her well in this field. To get her foot in the door, L'Huillier offered to intern to gain insider knowledge and to confirm her decision to leave behind a TV career. "After months of devoting one day a week to the PR department at The Vermont Teddy Bear Company—in addition to being a waitress at night and a full-time reporter—I convinced the powers that be at VTB they needed me and could obtain huge success with an additional PR person," says L'Huillier. They took her advice and within a year from when she was hired, L'Huillier was promoted to public relations manager not only for The Vermont Teddy Bear Company, but for their sister companies, too.

I Consult to Deepen My Expertise

Two years after a major career transition from teaching at a university in Minnesota to nonprofit management in New York, Norrine Russell, a psychologist with a specialization in girls' and women's development, discovered that consulting part-time is one of the best ways to network. She created a web page for herself, www.norrinerussell.com, so that if organizations were looking for someone with her expertise, Russell's name would be out there. "Consulting projects help me to develop new skills and become more well-known in my field, which I know will pay off in the future (and has already paid off in additional income!). When it's time to look for a new job, I'll now be able to network through all my consulting contacts and find something ideal."

I Mentor Other Women

"One of my contacts when I was in-house counsel was a very bright young woman who was working her way through law school and doing contract administration for one of my client groups. Recognizing that for her legal résumé, it would be beneficial to have some clerking experience, I persuaded her business unit to allow her to clerk for me in the legal department. She gained significant experience there," says Ann Newton, partner at Houston-based law firm Hayes and Boone. The mentoring paid off in spades, both personally and professionally. "I gained a fan and friend for many years, who has since generated several significant clients."

I Work the Yellow Pages

As a freshman engineering student, Irene Chang wanted to work for the summer but didn't know how to get a good job, especially since many companies don't recruit for engineering interns until after their junior year. After going through family contacts unsuccessfully, Chang whipped out the phone book and cold-called each one of the listed engineering firms. "Some were pretty quick to say that they had no opportunities," says Chang. "But there were a few that were at least pleasant. In the end, I got a summer job with one of them, who had never had an engineering intern before. In fact, I spent two summers there and even got a holiday bonus."

I Take to the Streets

"As a seasoned sales pro, I tired of my job at one of the largest worldwide overnight delivery services and I wanted to make a shift to a more intimate setting where I could be truly passionate about what I was selling," says Stephanie Biasi. Knowing that small businesses are the leading source of job creation, she cruised her neighborhood by foot to check out the potential opportunities in her own backyard. "I spotted a bright red neon sign that read 'Women For Hire' and it piqued my interest. Turns out that my timing couldn't have been better. The company was expanding quickly and needed a new account executive on the spot." Biasi has been with Women For Hire since 2000.

I'm Visible

"After launching my public relations practice, I attended an art auction and bid on a painting, competing with a gentleman who ultimately outbid me. When the bidding was over, he and I began talking. I told him that I had just gone into business for myself, and he asked for my card," says communications specialist Diane Pettus. "He called the next day, and I've been on retainer with his company for several years. He's also referred me to other businesses."

I Am Not Fearful

"Get over the fear by honestly asking yourself, 'What's the worst thing that can happen?' When I wanted to start my first company, I realized that the worst thing that would happen was that it might fail and I'd end up having to get a job to pay off some debt. Once I realized that wouldn't be the end of the world, I was able to go ahead and do it," says Donna Gent, president of Kinderstreet.com, an internet application for early childhood programs. "Every time you are faced with a decision that seems scary, get out a piece of paper and make a list of all the negative things that 'might' happen. Then make a list of the positive things. You will discover that your imagined fears are usually worse than anything in reality."

I Created a Prescription to Pave the Way for Others

"I felt fortunate to know at age eleven that I dreamed of being a physician. Women physicians were a rarity and I was told I'd probably never accomplish my ultimate goal. Through years of positive thinking, study, and unabashed perseverance, I continued to set out on my journey to carry out what I had set my heart to complete. I believed in my own strength and abilities, regardless of what others said was unattainable," says Dr. Dorothy Mitchell-Leef, a reproductive endocrinologist and infertility specialist. "That same persistence and energy helped me convince those in decision-making positions that I could be just as successful in performing surgery and delivering babies as the men in the field of obstetrics and gynecology. Knowing that the final outcome would be whether other women would be allowed to enter the same program, dependent on my accomplishments, continued to give me the strength to never falter in completing the difficult years ahead." Today Dr. Mitchell-Leef's Atlanta-based practice is among the nation's top clinics in this highly specialized field. "I have felt rewarded by seeing the number of women in OB/GYN now equal or in some areas exceed the number of men in the profession. I know that women, like myself, persisted and proved that we could accomplish similar goals previously held as commonplace by men. Saying 'yes' to challenges, no matter how daunting, continues to energize me today. Women must believe in themselves, accept that you might fail or fall short of your goal, but realize the journey can be as rewarding as the final outcome. Your successes, no matter how small, can be stepping-stones for others, to make significant advances for the future."

I Went Back to School

Suzanne Jenniches was the first and, for a decade, the only woman in the environmental engineering master's program at Johns Hopkins University. "The best career decision I made was going back and getting my engineering degree. I wish I had known about that when I was in high school. The first time I heard the word *engineer* was when I was twenty-three," says Jenniches, now an engineer at aerospace giant Northrop Grumman. Now this role model urges parents and students not to wait too long to think about engineering. "Think about it now as a career option."

I Don't Waste Time

"I remember reading a *Dear Abby* column years ago when a woman wrote in to say that she'd always wanted to be a nurse, and that she still wanted to be one," recalls Marilee Driscoll, a speaker on retirement issues and author of *The Complete Idiot's Guide to Long-term Care Planning*. "She was hesitant and said that if she went back to school she'd be fifty-three by the time she graduated. Abby's response was, 'How old will you be in four years if you don't go back to school?' Time passes whether we are accomplishing our goals and realizing our dreams or not. I use this advice often in making professional decisions, including the decision to get out of the insurance business and become a speaker and consultant."

I Believe in the Golden Rule

"As a freelancer, being in 'job hunt' mode is a way of life 24/7. I've found the secret is not in being smarter, more proficient in certain skills, or networking. Instead it's all about being a good person. Considerate. Treating everyone you work with like an actual person, and not a means to an assignment or promotion," says Sharon Naylor, author of fourteen books and hundreds of magazine articles. "Your reputation precedes you, and how you treat all others in every rung of an office builds or breaks your chances of success. I've had editors leave one magazine and recommend me to their colleagues following them in, because I'm a professional who does great work and I cultivate a friendly relationship with them all. A sense of humor and consideration are a welcome break for that working-like-a-dog assistant or multitasking editor."

I Bring Care to the Workplace

"By being a mother and a professional, I've learned that creating a family atmosphere in the workplace is the most successful tactic," says Gail G. Heyman, a dental hygienist in Atlanta, Georgia. "Just as you must understand the strengths and needs of your family, you need to understand the needs of your co-workers. Being friendly, honest, and accepting are some qualities that help create a cohesive team. Building positive relationships definitely makes your working experience more enjoyable and successful."

Simple strategies for getting ahead have worked for these women and just might work for you when applied at the right time and place. If you notice one thing about really successful women, they all have a will to succeed. We know from having started our own businesses and forged our own ways that determination, persistence, and an unfailing sense of confidence is essential for moving your career in a positive direction. Along with the lessons we've presented for getting ahead, we also know that it's a strong combination of what you know and who you know. Building those contacts, mentors, and advocates along the way will give you a boost that will catapult you to greater heights. We know you can do it and wish you the best in your journey to get ahead, stay ahead, and succeed beyond your dreams.

And to you, our reader, we say, hip, hip, hooray! We celebrate and congratulate you for taking your success seriously and doing everything within your power to shape your future and pave a career path that will lead you on a fulfilling journey to everything you deserve.

INDEX

ABOUT THE AUTHORS

Tory Johnson is the founder and CEO of Women For Hire (www.women-forhire.com), a business that produces career fairs connecting America's leading employers with smart, diverse women in all fields. Each year, Women For Hire events enable more than five hundred top employers to meet directly with more than thirty thousand high-caliber job-seekers at a time when workplace diversity is essential and recruiting is competitive.

Johnson conducts job-strategy seminars, lectures on networking, and coaches job-seekers on career development throughout the country. She is a frequent media guest on career issues and has appeared on CNBC, CNN, and numerous ABC, CBS, FOX, and NBC stations throughout the country. She has been featured in the *New York Times*, *Miami Herald*, *Atlanta Journal*, *Chicago Tribune*, and *Dallas Morning News*, among other coverage, providing extensive career advice.

Johnson is highly involved with all aspects of her business—managing staff, planning events, and personally inspiring the women she serves. Johnson's interest in empowering women and the development of her own self-confidence is traced back to high school in Miami Beach, where she and her partner became the first females in Florida to win several prestigious state debate titles. For three years Johnson spent every weekend competing in the male-dominated sport of traditional debate—no easy feat for a young woman. Since founding Women For Hire in 1999, Johnson has helped thousands of women find jobs that will start them on—or advance them in—successful professional career paths. She lives in New York City with her husband and three children.

Robyn Freedman Spizman (robynspizman.com) is an award-winning author and has written over seventy parenting, inspirational, and how-to books. She has authored *The GIFTionary: An A-to-Z Reference Guide for Solving Your Gift-Giving Dilemmas . . . Forever!*; *Make It Memorable: An A-Z Guide to Making Any Event, Gift, or Occasion . . . Dazzling!*; *When Words Matter Most*; *The Thank-You Book*; and is the coauthor of *Getting Through to Your Kids*; *300 Incredible Things for Women on the Internet*; and *Good Behavior*. She has reported for the past twenty years as a consumer advocate on many how-to topics from saving time and getting organized to gift-giving and the hottest products for Atlanta NBC affiliate WXIA-TV in her popular "Been There, Bought That" weekly segment and on Atlanta's Star 94 with *The GIFTionary*. Spizman has also been featured as a guest on over 10,000 leading national and local television talk and radio shows including NBC's *Today,* CNN, CNNfn, the Discovery Channel, and the Oxygen Network, and her advice and books have appeared in many national publications including the *New York Times, Cosmopolitan, Woman's Day, Family Circle, Redbook, Parents, Child,* and *USA Today*. A well-known speaker, Spizman has spoken to thousands of women across the country and was named one of Atlanta's top Divas in Business by *Business to Business* magazine. She lives in Atlanta with her husband and two children.

CONTACT WOMEN FOR HIRE
AND THE AUTHORS

Nothing makes us happier and more proud than hearing from women who've found a nugget or two of success from our efforts. Since the 2002 publication of our first book, *Women For Hire: The Ultimate Guide to Getting a Job,* we have received thousands of emails from women who shared their stories after applying some of our advice. Email us at book@womenforhire.com.

Please visit **womenforhire.com** to register for our free email newsletter filled with the latest job search tips and information on who's hiring. You'll learn about our coaching services and seminars, and you can get dates and locations for our upcoming Women For Hire events throughout the country, which are free for job-seekers and provide excellent networking opportunities.